Consistent Creative Content

A Guide to Authoring and Blogging in the Social Media Age

By Lee Hall

Text Copyright March 2021

© 2021, Lee Hall, except as provided by the Copyright Act January 2015 no part of this publication may be reproduced, stored in a retrieval system or transmitted in any form or by any means without the prior written permission of the Author and Publisher.

About the Author

LEE HALL IS A best-selling independently published author and blogger from the UK. His works include *The Teleporter, The Ghost Beside Me* and the occult *Order of the Following* series. When he isn't writing Lee spends much of his time reading fellow indie authors works while doing his best to support them through blogging. You can catch him on Twitter most days trying to be witty.

This book is dedicated to anyone who has ever delved into the world of creative writing. Even if you've simply strung a few sentences together all the way to writing a full-length novel and everyone in between; our struggle unites us.

Contents

About the Author   *iii*

Introduction   *1*

Blogging: The Basics   *5*

    The Basics of Blogging
    The Basics of Blog Content
    Basic Blog Content Ideas
    The Anatomy of a Blog Post

Social Media: The Basics   *17*

    The Tweet Machine Basics for Authors and Bloggers
    Facebook Basics for Authors and Bloggers
    Instagram Basics for Authors
    Goodreads for Authors and Bloggers
    BookBub for Authors and Bloggers

Authoring: The Basics   *26*

    Basic Authoring… for Authors
    Basic Authoring: Publishing Overview
    Avoiding Scams
    Managing Time

Book Production   *38*

    Book Production: The Modern Wonder of Publishing
    Book Production: The Basic Anatomy of a Book

> Book Production: Get Yourself an Editor

Book Marketing Basics:
A Memoir and Roadmap   *45*

> Book Marketing Basics: The Truth and a Memoir
> Book Marketing Basics: Do the Work: A Roadmap to Consistent Content
> The Highs, Lows and Many Different Struggles: Was it worth it?

Book Marketing: Selling and Promotion   *64*

> Book Marketing: The Art of Indirect Selling for Authors and Bloggers
> Book Marketing: Pricing
> Book Marketing: Promotion Basics
> Book Marketing: Book Promotion Methods: Everyone Loves a Freebie
> Book Marketing: Book Promotion Methods: Mailing lists
> Book Marketing: Book Promotion Methods: Paid Advertising
> Book Marketing: Book Promotion Methods: Free Advertising
> Book Marketing: Book Promotion Methods: Miscellaneous Free Advertising
> Book Promotion: The Book Launch

Book Marketing:
Book Promotion Worked Examples   *95*

> Book Promotion Worked Examples: Putting the theory into Practice
> Book Promotion Worked Examples

Book Reviews   *115*

> Book Reviews: Overview

Book Reviews: Preparing One's Mind and Dealing with Negativity
Book Reviews: The Business of Reviews
Book Reviews: Getting More Reviews
Book Reviews: How to Write a Great One

Built for Success:
Turning the corner in Authoring and Blogging   *130*

Built for Success: A Major Turning Point
Catching That Wave: Tracking Success

Advanced Authoring and Blogging   *139*

Advanced Authoring and Blogging: Dealing with Toxicity
Advanced Authoring and Blogging: Preserving your Mental Health
Advanced Tweet Machine Methods
Advanced Blogging Methods
Advanced Authoring: Tracking Results

Conclusion: Everything I have learned   *153*

The Conclusion: A Summary for your Reference
The Conclusion: Everything I have Learned

Thanking Those Who Shaped This Journey   *163*

Authors Note   *165*

Introduction

THIS BOOK EXPLORES WHAT I've learnt on my publishing journey, presenting it in a way that I hope will inspire you to believe in your own abilities to replicate and even surpass my success. Belief is all you really need on any journey and if I can get results that I'm happy with, then you certainly can. Success is based upon how you judge the results of something over time – it's both fickle and in the eye of the beholder.

I've always measured my results beside the number from where I started – absolute zero. And compared to zero my numbers today appear to be quite impressive, but the truth is, they haven't always been like that. I've spent most of my time nearer to zero than any other number and that's something everyone must be prepared to face. Some call low numbers failure but to me there are no failures in life, just lessons and opportunity. Both go hand in hand when it comes to writing. The most important thing in writing is to start, even if it is at zero.

This guide can be defined as a series of experiences from the many years I've spent as both a blogger and an author in the social media age. Much of the content might seem obvious but there is also some advice I have never shared before. My hope is to help you progress in the world of authoring and blogging even if you take just one sentence of advice from all of this; to me that'll be a good job done. Like I said, this may just be in the eye of the beholder –

you, and you alone can go as far as the imagination will allow.

Before we go any further, I will tell you now that this book is for anyone looking for advice and inspiration in blogging and book writing. You could already have an established blog or a backlist of books written and published. You might even be pondering your very first foray into the world of words. Everyone is welcome here and you'll find something, no matter where you're starting from. Much of it is delivered from the perspective of a beginner with some of the advanced stuff being advice I follow every day.

For me, writing books and blogging go hand in hand and while they are both explored in detail, you won't find any information on how to specifically write and format a book or construct a blog site. I am not qualified to show you the latter and the former… well, nobody can formally teach you *how* to write a book in my opinion. It is my belief that the journey of writing and finishing a book is something only the individual can find within themselves. Instead, we will explore how to market yourself as a creator on social media through all the various channels I have experienced. At times it will mainly be blog-centric, but there are some in-depth marketing resources for authors as well. Many of the chapters ahead are interwoven with blogging and authoring advice because to me, they go, hand in hand.

I have started in this manner for two reasons:

1. So anyone can see from previewing the first pages if it could be of help to them;
2. To be upfront about what success I have had in blogging – see the graph below.

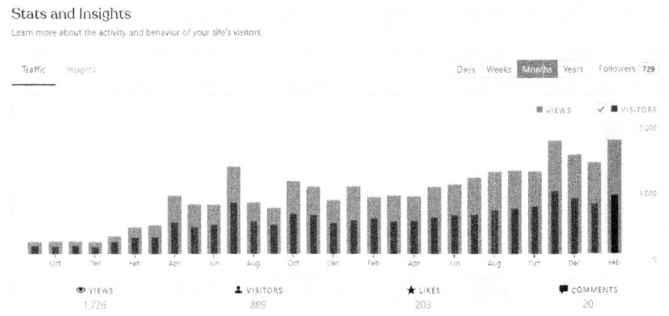

This graph shows my blog viewing numbers over many months from September 2018 to recent times. As you can see, they gradually and progressively improved over time forming into a 'wave' which will be explored further ahead. The blogging element of this book will focus on how I got to those numbers and how I took the opportunity to continually improve them. The graph stands as proof that everything you write gets results to some extent, and those results echo the message that everything else in this book will take time and that there are no quick fixes.

I say results because for me these things worked; there is no guarantee that they will work for you. I'm in the inspiration business not the miracle business, but every wordsmith faces different circumstances and so I have concluded that, across the board, you need three core attributes to have any chance of success in blogging and authoring:

1. You need to be **consistent**;
2. You need to be **creative**; and
3. You need **content**.

This trio is the main reason why my blogging and authoring endeavours have been successful. Because I hold these attributes in such high regard I even included them in the title of this book.

In some applications you'll only need one of the trio, in others two and there are a few more vital attributes outside the trio that I will point out along the way. Some, until now, were my best kept secrets while others appear obvious.

All in all, this guide is laced with ideas that'll help you improve your authoring and blogging, to achieve greater success. Many of the sections will even begin with snippets of advice from the various authors, bloggers, creators and friends I have connected with over the years – all of whom have found success in their own ways.

Apart from blog views or book sales what else counts as success? Follow my words and I will show you. Remember, you can do what I've done and go even further.

Blogging: The Basics

"Don't ever feel alone, embrace the book community, find blogs that interest you and comment on them, you can make so many friendships that way, also don't be afraid to ask questions."

– Blair Leftly, book reviewer and blogger.
(Feed the Crime Blog)

The Basics of Blogging

To SPEAK AND RAMBLE incessantly without interruption is just one of the many definitions I use for blogging. It's an opportunity to create your own corner of the internet and speak about whatever subject you wish. Blogging is a great outlet to extend your personality or be someone else entirely while it can also be the home to your very own brand.

Branding is probably the first fundamental basic of blogging and by that I mean choosing a title for it. This is your opportunity to be creative. Back when I started some years ago, the gimmick or a play on words style title was popular, so I eventually settled for *'Lee's Hall of Information'*. It's important to relate your blog name to your subject matter so potential readers know straight away what your blog will be about. *'Lee's Hall of Information'* doesn't exactly give much away so I added the tag line, *'A blog and journey towards publication'*, which eventually evolved to what it reads now: *'A blog and journey in publishing'*. You won't have to look far in the world of blogging to find some wonderful titles many creatives have used.

Make it memorable, make it unique and make it stand out.

There are a stack of different easy-to-use blog hosting sites out there. I chose WordPress for its functionality and easy to use accessibility. WordPress is also great for the social element of blogging and everyone has their own unique feed, which fills up after time with blog posts from those you follow. In the earlier stages of my foray into blogging, this helped push my posts out towards new readers as the feed also includes suggested blogs to follow.

After watching a few self-help videos, I was able to put together something that represented a decent-looking site (in the eyes of the beholder anyway). Over the years WordPress has grown and can now support the most basic of sites all the way to something more extravagant. You can choose to pay for a particular URL or just keep the free package – all of this depends on how much you are willing to invest. As a rule, the more you invest the better it is, and with WordPress your money is safe. For me, I started with a free package until such time as any type of growth could persuade me otherwise. Even today I don't pay for a lot, just the dot-com URL.

So, you've got a snappy or witty name for your blog and it is clear to potential readers what your subject matter is all about, you've chosen a hosting site, and put together a nice shiny looking page with colours and a menu that doesn't have a lot of options. In the beginning I had two menu sections other than the blog: 'Contact' and 'About'. You'll grow more, I'm sure. Now it's time to think about content.

The Basics of Blog Content

I INITIALLY STARTED MY blog as an outlet for writing and to grow a social media presence. This was when the wide-eyed dream of finding a literary agent to publish my less than sub-par writing fuelled everything I did. This was going to be effortless and flawless all at once. Big time Hollywood producers would be calling me in the morning and that six-figure advance would soon get wired into my bank account. Of course, I've woken up since then and over the years I've come to realise a dream like that is still a long way away. It's possibly closer now, but either way it's still a dream that I'm working towards. (Inspiration, not miracles).

To achieve anything worthwhile in this life I have discovered you need to roll up your sleeves and work for it. With blogging and writing this is the same, in this social media age the opportunity is out there; you just need to go and grab it!

From the very beginning of putting my Hall of Information Blog together, I had in mind what content was going to be produced. This would consist of introducing myself and what I am all about while also laying out to my potential readers what my blog and writing intended to achieve with my blog and other writing in the long term. Of course, this is easier said than done – even now I am unsure what my writing has achieved. It takes a lot of time for this to become clear and it is important to consider your writing endeavours a long-term investment but remember: **starting is the most important thing**. It may feel like nobody is listening to you blog into an empty void, but we all start somewhere. Being able to think of subjects that'll make compelling blog posts is another hurdle – we'll cover that soon.

Now before we go any further, this is one of those 'moments'. You know, an important attribute outside of the trio type of moment. And it is this:

In blogging and writing, set yourself realistic, achievable goals while also managing your expectations.

Translation: Rome was not built in a day.

My expectations were mostly unknown while bordering on trying not to be disappointed. At the time I had a social media presence on both Facebook and Twitter, though my following was much lower than today's numbers. In essence I was taking a plunge into the unknown – as creators that leap of faith is something we can't avoid. It's both scary and exciting and if you feel neither towards anything in this life, then is it worthwhile? All I wanted was a few folks to take a look and care about what I was saying and to build a following who would eventually read my books.

With that in mind, I put together my first ever blog post, simply called 'Pilot', which did what I set out to do. A handful of people clicked 'Like' on the post and some even commented. For me it made my first ever foray into blogging feel like a massive success.

The statistics at the time my first post got published were as follows:

Views: 29
Post Likes: 5
Comments: 3

To some these numbers may seem small, but to me they meant everything and they still do. Success is in the eye of the beholder and when it comes to writing and blogging you are only competing against yourself.

My longer-term plan was to write a series of posts that continued to introduce myself, my goals and what I was all about. Each one would be published weekly and kept in line with the all-important attributes of being consistent and creative while I continued to find ways to (try and) entertain and inform readers. This beginner level content resulted in 7 regular posts that baby stepped me into the world of creating content, but I can only speak about myself so much, so I needed to find other subjects to blog about.

Basic Blog Content Ideas

Even though the Hall of Information was a blog and journey in publishing, it wasn't always going to be about that, and the more diverse your content, the higher chance that passing trade will read it. Now this may contradict my initial advice about branding, but you are the creative boss in all this and diversity in content is sometimes a good thing. In my case, at the time I was writing science fiction books which are yet to see the light of day, so I needed separate consistent creative content that casual readers could just pick up. More importantly, I needed to write posts that a wide array of readers could relate to.

This can be quite a hurdle for some and might take organisation, depending on how creative you are. Thinking of what subjects could possibly be appealing and compelling for a reader is a challenge. These days, while I have some structure, my ability to think on my feet has improved. As an author who writes with no real plan I've become adept at 'making it up as I go along' when it comes to some of my blog content. This method isn't for everyone and it wasn't always that way for me either. If you do adopt that method, your ability will improve over time by the act of doing – like all writing.

Over the next few years after that first blog post I managed to channel my interests and experiences of life into content. While I did continue to blog about writing and pondering whether I should self-publish, the Hall of Information still needed to operate regularly and be able to reach out to a wider audience.

Readers don't always want to hear about one thing, variety is a key factor in producing consistent creative content.

It's easy for me to say consistent creative content but what am I actually referring to? Although these may appear obvious, here is a list of basic blog content ideas that will reach wider audiences:

Introducing yourself in a creative and fun way;
Book Recommendations;
Current Movie Reviews;
Classic Movie Reviews;
Movie Previews;
Television Show Reviews;
Television Show Recommendations;
Video Game Reviews;
Day's out/experience Reviews;
Food and Nutrition Reviews;
Product Reviews;
Exercise Regime Reviews;
Politics*;

Current Events;
Mental health and self-care;
Cosplay;
Poetry;
How to Tutorials;
Regular Diary Style Posts;
Book Reviews.

I have highlighted the last two because back when I began blogging there were two subjects I did not think much about or even cover yet proved instrumental to the success of my blogging endeavours and wider writing career. If done right they can also be highly social and being social is at the centre of most blogging.

My Weekly Ramble blog post is a regular diary style account in a few hundred words of what's currently going through my mind or a reflection of what's happening in the world. It's written in a way where each entry stands alone and over the years I have covered many subjects, from receiving less than satisfactory book reviews to the advantages of being a part of the wider writing community. It's an opportunity to blog, vent and hopefully reach someone who cares. It's also written in an inclusive way so I confide in my reader – including others is a fun way of still talking about yourself without feeling guilty or being boring. My weekly ramble post is normally the best viewed article of the week.

Book reviews are something I have dedicated a whole section to further on and trust me, it's a key part of my blogging.

*When it comes to politics and heavy opinion, these are subjects I would advise you steer clear from early on. There are prolific bloggers out there who thrive off controversial subject matters and for those with a smaller following this sort of practice will only hurt that. Heavy opinion/political pieces also attract attention that may not be the type you want, if you want to sell books or get regular views.

The Anatomy of a Blog Post

THE TRUTH IS, I can't physically teach you to write a blog post or guarantee anyone will read it, but I can show you what a post should look like from examples that have seen results. Much of the blogging advice I have given so far is broad but now it's time to get into the nitty-gritty detail.

First and foremost, you need a gripping title. Much like a newspaper headline, it needs to grab passers-by and tell folks what it's about. This is entirely dependent on your subject but it's also an opportunity to be creative.

One of my all-time most viewed blog posts is titled: 'DDP YOGA REVIEW'

You can probably guess what it's about and while it may not be writing related, some of my top read posts aren't.

> ***Top Tip:*** Reviewing/blogging about something that is continually rising in popularity may lead to guaranteed reads over an extended period of time.

Next you're going to need an appealing opening statement that immediately hooks readers in. Most of my post introductions are also formatted in header text and bold these days. The first few sentences are extremely important in setting the tone while relaying information to potential readers. If you have a blog feed like the WordPress reader, the first few sentences will appear as a preview to your followers so it's imperative to hook them in with it. When you share this post across social media some platforms will include a thumbnail image and text from the opening statement so it's important to consider that.

If we look at the post mentioned above and it's first few lines, they read like this:

'So here it is, my full review of DDP yoga! I have reached the conclusion of the beginner's schedule under Phase 1 and I am ready to share with the world my results and thoughts.'

Another example can be taken from my popular 2020 post 'Let's talk about... Book Marketing':

'Do you feel slightly dirty whenever you spam the link to your book on social media?'

As you can see, this introduction sets a certain comedic tone while also being relatable to authors. Of course, it's a question, which is great for engagement but all for the purpose of delivering it's message while attempting to be entertaining (hopefully) at the same time. For this post the audience was more specific (authors), so I wrote for that audience.

Another popular post which carried some controversial tones was from my Weekly Ramble series and began like this:

'I find myself resisting the urge to react to a negative review of The Teleporter.'

I've mentioned the subject of controversy before, and the post that followed this introduction garnered a positive reaction from the extended writing community/my following. Sometimes, if you conduct yourself in a decent way as an author or blogger, peers will jump to your defence in some instances. Normally I don't blog or write about deeply controversial subjects but every now and then they get a reaction. Now I did not directly respond to a negative review of my book *The Teleporter* but I did vent my feelings through this post. It's okay to vent feelings and confide in your following. Your blog is your space first and foremost. Sometimes if the situation aligns, loyal followers will swoop in to support you; they did for me and I even got a few book sales and reviews for it.

To briefly recap, your blog post should have a clear and concise title, it should then have a hooking introduction or an appealing opening statement. Next comes the subject matter – the body of the post. Your review, essay, story or whatever subject matter should fill this space in whatever way you like. Depending on that subject I recommend you allow some space for relevant pictures or artwork. You can find free stock images through Creative Commons websites like Pixabay, even if your subject is fictional, break the space between lots of writing with these. The ease of this may vary by blog provider I now tend to format the pictures centrally in each post with text above and below as opposed to having text beside. In this way when your post is viewed on a smaller screen the text doesn't get jumbled together on one side in a fine mess. People are reading more on smartphones and smaller screens, attention spans are getting shorter and pictures make for a nice addition.

It's important to be inclusive when writing a blog post. Extend the bridge to readers by using 'we' or 'us'. Refer to them, make the reader feel like they are next to you. Inclusion leads to engagement, engagement leads to reads and followers, followers become loyal and come back, some even invest in your work if it's for sale. Sales eventually lead to reviews. One day you could be satisfied with things… (this book does not guarantee such…)

When you've reached the end of a post it's now important to have some kind of sign off or call to action. This provides something to further include the reader while also engaging in them. Encourage your reader to leave a comment, thank them for reading and give them a reason to engage. The easiest way to stir engagement is to sign off with a question.

'What did you think loyal reader?'

'What's your experience with this well-known brand?'

'Thanks for reading, what do you think? Comments welcome.'

'How are you feeling today? My comments are open.'

And lastly, in order for your post to have some visibility I recommend inserting relevant tags and hashtags in addition to putting the post in a relevant category – this is dependent yet again on your provider. After some years I've built up quite a few categories and the tags I use relate to what the post is about. Popular tags I use are:

Book Review, Inspiration, Indie Books, Lee Hall, blogger, books, fun, inspire, imagine.

Popular hashtags I use are:

#bookreview #indiebooks #inspiration #feelings #blog #amwriting

Using different tags as much as possible will increase your chance of visibility from new readers.

Now you've put the blog post together an important and probably overlooked step is to finally proofread your work. The more you write, the better your eye will get for spotting simple spelling errors. Ask a close friend to take a read, some browsers will have an automatic spell check – spell checkers are not to be fully trusted unfortunately.

The final step in proofreading is to see how the post actually looks. WordPress allows bloggers to preview a post and to see what it will look like once live; this is quite a useful tool and something not to be overlooked.

Now you've done all of the above, you are nearly ready to hit publish but another important factor outside the trio beckons, timing.

For those just starting out it might be a little challenging to gauge when the bulk of your audience are online, but **timing** is everything for visibility. If you publish a blog post late at night, or even early in the morning, there's a likelihood it'll pass your readers/followers by. My blanket advice is to time your blog posts to release in the middle of the day – what time do I class as the middle of the day? 12:00PM GMT is my personal choice because I am in the UK, but there will be certain time zones that may miss out so this will be a personal preference. Gauge your audience. Even through trial and error you'll notice when your content gets more views. Try a few different times over different posts. This is why it's important to share the link after publishing your blog post at different times of the day via your social media channels.

In conclusion, the anatomy of a blog post should have the following attributes:

- A gripping title.
- An appealing opening statement.
- Subject matter.
- Relevant pictures or artwork.
- Inclusive.
- Sign off or call to action.
- Relevant tags.
- Proofread.
- Timing with relation to publishing and sharing the link.

Social Media: The Basics

"If you want to be a writer, then you need to write. It's not supposed to be easy, nothing good is easy. Just keep putting one word in front of the other."

– J.C. Lynch, blogger.
(Thinking Moon Blog)

The Tweet Machine Basics for Authors and Bloggers

THE WORLD OF SOCIAL media is the glue that holds all of my authoring and blogging efforts together. In particular, Twitter is a weird and wonderful vessel that sails the seas of social media and can be used as a valuable tool in both marketing and finding your own crowd. Everything I've learned from the Tweet machine can both be applied to all writers and bloggers who make up the wider writing community.

To begin with, my advice for any prospective writer or blogger is to get yourself a Twitter account. The potential reach you can achieve doesn't compare to anywhere else, so if you aren't on Twitter you will most probably struggle to reach potential readers.

You're going to need a handle (username). This can be creative or simple. Both work fine and yet again another important attribute outside of the trio looms.

To give yourself the best possible chance at Twitter success you need to be **honest**, **friendly** and **decent**. Why, you say? Because that's how I got several thousand followers in just a few years, so you need:

A real profile picture of yourself;

A friendly bio that describes who you are, what you do. The more inviting, fun and friendly the better;

A pinned Tweet – a tweet you can put at the top of your profile that relays what you currently have available/currently writing, what's coming soon or even a link to your book or blog;

To engage with others by commenting, offering help and advice, being friendly, supportive and decent;

To be honest. Trust me most twitter types are drawn it.

This also includes a following strategy that consists of:

Following those who follow you;

Unfollowing those who no longer follow you;

Following those who interest you.

Now you might be asking what exactly do I tweet about? My mantra is to tweet about anything as long as it informs, inspires, entertains or provides some level of value – this will normally lead to some engagement but if not it's probably due to lack of visibility because of a low follower count. I will typically add at least one hashtag to that tweet also.

Popular hashtags for authors and bloggers include: #author #writer #blogger #writingcommunity #amwriting #amreading.

Twitter is a wonderful arena full of folks just like you, and together the voice of authors and bloggers is louder trust me.

For absolute beginners it might feel like nobody is listening or seeing your posts. This is only reflective of your current following. At the very beginning tweet less and spend more time commenting on the tweets of others. Explore hashtags and search for folks who you have a common interest with.

Twitter takes some time and effort to work out and has a very specific psychology to master. As long as you are approachable and lightly social, you'll be okay but remember, it takes time and above all, good conversation between you and others. Before you experience any type of external success (book sales/blog views) your audience will need to feel like they can trust you. This can only be achieved long term and through genuine interactions. I call this the 'Algorithm of Trust'.

We shall explore Twitter in more detail later on, along with some advanced strategies. The most basic advice I can offer would be to take a look at your recent tweets. If they have a low amount of engagement then tweet less about these subjects; if there is higher engagement, do more of this. Eventually and if you keep to the strategy and mantra above, followers will arrive. Dive in and have fun connecting with others from all over the world!

Facebook Basics for Authors and Bloggers

FACEBOOK USED TO BE a much bigger and popular force in the social media world. My first social media platform just happened to be the Facebook page which launched in 2013. Over the years it has slipped down to possibly last place in all of my social media efforts. Most of my reasoning for that isn't my choice; other platforms have overtaken Facebook since and my experience is that there are now better places for social engagement and therefore obtaining results.

At the time of writing. Facebook remains popular among older users, but generally not so much when it comes to younger folks. That, however, is based solely upon my own experience. Over the years Facebook has seen a few controversies which may or may not have something to do with this.

That said, as an author Facebook has been very good for me and quite possibly represents a missed opportunity to sell a lot more books than I have done. People are the real power on this platform, so the more people you are friends with, the more chance you have at successfully launching a page. Then, when you launch that page, putting out regular content is key.

When I launched my page I invited most of my friends to 'Like' it and slowly but surely the following grew. When users 'Like' a page, posts will show up in their news feeds unless they choose to turn off that function. In theory the more 'Likes' a page has the more users will see a post. Today there are folks that only follow me via Facebook so it's a small slice of a potential marketing opportunity, but all social media outlets are an opportunity if used effectively.

I've never fully explored the concept of Facebook groups, which bring people from all over the world together. My advice would be to join as many relevant groups as possible while adopting the same philosophy as being on the Tweet machine. There are plenty of authors who have sold many books through Facebook (including me), and even if it isn't as powerful as before, most folks still log in to Facebook every day – so as an author and blogger I recommend you launch a page and begin sharing content. The platform still carries a lot of opportunity.

Family and friends are a great initial group to get support from and will help in spreading your words, but the beauty of all social media is that you never know who you might reach. My first novel *Open Evening* was only successful because of my Facebook friends and it was the foothold that paved my way forward.

It took nearly seven years for my page to reach 500 plus Likes, but considering I began at zero – and after everything the platform has been through – I shall take that as a win.

Selling books through a Facebook following will be explored further in the book promotion section but my tips for beginners would be to take it slow. Post regularly but not constantly. Facebook can be strict if you share a link too many times and I tend to post anything after midday (UK time), when I know the majority of my audience will be online. It's important to know your audience and know when they are online – **timing** comes to mind again.

One or two likes for a post is more than a win because that's what I get even now at the best of times. Pages are also a great way to connect with other authors who are on the same team as you in this. Like their pages and if you conduct yourself well, they will return the favour.

Your own private Facebook profile is also a great place to share content and get the attention of the friends and family who you will need to begin with.

Instagram Basics for Authors

IF THE MAJORITY OF younger folks don't use Facebook too often, then where do they go? A slice of the younger social media demographic spend their time on Instagram, which is powered by Facebook and makes for an incredibly useful tool to market just about anything. The focus on Instagram is mainly visual, with users sharing either pictures or video content via their profile which is then relayed onto their feed.

Personally, I use Instagram's story function more than anything, which is a big opportunity for direct engagement by sharing video and visual content directly to followers. When something is added to the story function it is only visible for 24 hours. Often I run a poll or ask my following questions to stir some engagement or I share a screenshot of my latest blog post and leave the link in my profile bio.

Only every now and then do I post a new picture or video to my main feed. My following, although consistent, hasn't grown much over the years, so I use Instagram as the platform that sits between Twitter and Facebook just to ensure further coverage. Hashtags are a must for wider reach and commenting on other followers' content should never be overlooked.

Goodreads for Authors and Bloggers

WHILE DRAFTING THIS BOOK, I initially left out Goodreads because it can be a polarising subject to some. With that opinion to one side there is no doubt it's a useful and powerful platform for both authors and book reviewers alike if used in the right way.

For the beginner, consider Goodreads to be the Facebook for books; it's a place for readers to leave reviews and for authors to list their works and create profiles. There aren't many higher profile book-specific social media platforms around and for that it can be a useful tool. Those who are either in the book-blogging or authoring camps will benefit from using Goodreads because most higher profile folks use it.

Specifically, I use it to list the books I intend to review – this is a handy and vital way to stay organised. I also have my own books listed along with an author profile. This is something I recommend you do, so reviewers and readers can find them. If your work can be found on Goodreads then it can then be listed 'to read' by users, which may eventually lead to a sale or review. Very often I forget which books I've intended to read, so having a list to consult is essential for book reviewers.

An often-overlooked part of Goodreads is the social element and specifically the groups. From author circles to those looking to review certain genres, chances are there is a group for whatever specialist interest you have in books.

It's easy enough to create a profile as Goodreads is linked to most major social media platforms.

BookBub for Authors and Bloggers

OFTEN UNHEARD BY INDIE authors and bloggers is the highly regarded bargain book promotion site BookBub, who advertise a plethora of discounted or free books every day to millions of email subscribers. Their reach is often considered the highest available. While BookBub celebrate the fact they support indie authors, they also advertise some very well-known traditionally-published names in the industry. They tend to promise the highest standard of books and from experience they also have the highest standard of readers.

In my opinion BookBub is a great platform to leave book reviews and advertise my efforts as an author so it can be beneficial to both authors and bloggers alike. I would recommend that any author signs up and creates a profile. From there you can list your books and they can be reviewed by prospective readers. This is the basic requirement if you want to explore their extensive advertising packages and of course apply for the Featured Deal – more about that below.

For bloggers, particularly of the book review persuasion, BookBub is great platform to post your reviews on and further connect with authors. As long as the book you've reviewed has been uploaded to BookBub by the author, there's nothing stopping you putting that review up to help spread the word about your efforts and their book.

BookBub Featured Deal

The BookBub Featured Deal is considered the 'Holy Grail' of book advertisements by authors in the know and I would agree with that bold statement. A Featured Deal taps into the huge email following of BookBub, so to have your work featured will near enough guarantee some level of return, whether that's a profit or at least covers the cost of the promotion. From experience, getting a featured deal was a major turning point in my efforts as an author. BookBub are strict and only select certain books. It is incredibly hard to persuade them to feature your work, and their selection process is based on quality, among other things. Having somehow been featured twice, my advice is to keep applying until they say yes while having a book with a certain specialist niche will increase your chances of being selected. If you have a backlist of books this will also help, along with an engaged social media following and some ratings for your works. If you do manage to secure a featured deal, prepare to have many more eyes on your work than ever before.

Top Tip: Just looking at BookBub's front page will give you an indication of what type of reads they are currently choosing. If yours fits within their current choices, you may have a better chance at being selected by them.

Authoring: The Basics

"It's going to be an incredibly challenging, difficult and unpredictable road, but you can definitely succeed if you never give up."

– Marc Cavella,
author of Tabernacle and The Ballad of Ricky Risotto.

Basic Authoring… for Authors

While blogging and social media are huge pillars of my efforts, writing books has been just as prevalent and important to everything else. While it is my belief that no one can teach you to write a book or a story, there is no denying that there are many professionals who can guide you in spelling, grammar, punctuation and every other nut and bolt of the English language. That is without mentioning the importance of editors.

Storytelling, for me, has always had a level of spirituality that you have to find within and book writing has been defined by many generations, from the classic authors all the way to the modern day. One word which gets used quite a lot is 'subjective' – meaning there are no actual right or wrong answers and no good or bad, because it all of depends on opinion, taste and personal experience. Writing is a type of creativity where even rules can be questioned much of the time, especially for the sake of artistic licence. As I said, to me much of writing has no formal way of being taught.

If I were to define it, writing is the **translation** of imagination and thought onto the page through the mode of words.

Simple enough?

The translation of what you see in your head into written word is something you can only get better at by doing. The more hours you dedicate to staring at that half-filled page, desperately trying to figure out how to extract your thoughts into words, the easier it will become.

From heart, to mind, to hand to pen – the journey of our imagination is a long but rewarding one if you dedicate time to it.

But how do you actually tell a story, you ask? All of my writing efforts have been inspired by stories or moments that meant something to me in life. My advice is to draw your own inspiration from the things that speak to you – from real life to movies, plays, music, and of course, books. Just think of a time in your life or a scene that meant something and try to capture it in your own writing efforts. Pay tribute to those moments of real things and remember most importantly to capture the sense of feeling, because if your reader feels something then you've got them hooked. Using all five senses will capture that feeling.

For complete novices, writing might feel tiring to begin with. It may feel like your energy is being zapped after just an hour of figuring this whole thing out, your throat might be dry after, you could even lose colour in your face and feel weak. Have you got the shakes and all of a sudden feel lethargic? All of these symptoms are normal when it comes to writing, especially at the beginning. I know because that's exactly how I've felt and, the only way to keep these feelings at bay is to build up a resistance to them by putting in the time.

I won't insult your intelligence by asking if you want to be a writer: of course you do; you took the time and most probably paid some hard-earned money to buy this book. Having done that, you must have decided, on some level, that you want this. I believe you, and you can do it. It won't be easy, but you're unlikely to be deterred. I believe that, too. Why? Because you wouldn't have bothered to even look for a book like this, let alone take the time to read it.

If you are prepared to **dedicate time** toiling away at your masterpiece there will come a feeling of solitary existence and perhaps even loneliness. This is just an unfortunate sacrifice you will have to make, because only you can write the story or stories you want to write. Loneliness is just a side effect of this journey and while many writers claim to be introverts, that's normally because we enjoy writing and have to be alone for it.

You will also have to learn the deepest level of **patience**, to the point of it being a discipline. This applies throughout the whole process from having an idea, to writing it, editing and everything the comes after – the publishing and the dealing with anything external. Stay cool, stay calm and take your time. Patience really is a virtue and the true sign of professionalism in authoring. This also comes into play while marketing yourself as a personality online. Those with tact and patience eventually attract the right attention.

Above everything in writing books, they are just words and sometimes that's all they need to be seen as.

What now?

Deciding to take the plunge into writing a book is both brave and only the beginning. Let's say you've now done that, which is by no means a small thing. Let's skip ahead because preparation for the future is just as vital to writing in this journey.

You've figured out how to **translate** your thoughts onto that page, you've **dedicated** hours to writing it and been very **patient** with the whole deal. Somehow, you've got to those two words every author always aims for, 'The End', but congratulations: that's just the starting line and the shiny vessel that is your author persona has just pulled up to begin the race. The vehicle is your content. Even though much of the content that follows is for authors with a completed book there is nothing better than being prepared, so even if you haven't finished that masterpiece, there's plenty for you to take in.

No matter what your intentions are going forward it's time to start marketing yourself as an author. There are a host of social media platforms and subsequent guides that lie ahead in this book, and you'll find specific advice for them. There is no right or wrong way to do any of this. You could already have established a social media presence while writing or you could have taken the plunge into blogging (which I highly recommend you do). For the purposes of this section, we're going to look into the book side of things specifically because soon enough you are going to face something of a fork in the writing road: Just how are you going to publish this masterpiece?

Basic Authoring: Publishing Overview

IN SIMPLE TERMS THERE are two main ways in which you'll be able to hold that published book in your hands: Traditional Publishing or Self/Independent Publishing.

Traditional Publishing

Traditional Publishing normally consists of querying literary agents – or editors directly, though this practice is becoming increasingly outdated – usually with a sample of with your completed, polished and edited manuscript. Note the importance of this; you really should have the completed manuscript ready to go upon request, and always check an agent or publisher's genre preferences and submissions guidelines If an agent likes your work they will agree to represent you and then pitch it to larger scale publishers. One of these publishing houses may then agree to take on or buy your work and publish it.

This is just a very brief overlook of Traditional Publishing, it was the route I first pursued, albeit without success despite querying over a hundred agents. This is where I learned to be patient. It's extremely difficult to attract the attention of a literary agent and convince them to represent you, even if they do there's still no guarantee of getting published but it isn't impossible. It can be time consuming, waiting to hear back from agents you've queried, and it's very unlikely a beginner author will successfully traditionally publish unless you have a very unique set of circumstances. There will always be exceptional cases and a big lesson for me was finding out that I wasn't one. Saying that, there is no harm in trying, and if you research agents and do your homework it could be your lucky day, but manage your expectations!

Larger publishers typically no longer accept unsolicited works from unknown or debut authors, preferring to deal only with agents instead. Since agents constantly receive queries in large quantities, they sometimes never get back to you or they will at least take a while. But I reiterate, there are always exceptions. Either way, by following the 'Trad Pub' route, it will take a huge amount of time from your initial query to getting to hold the published book in your hands.

The good news is that there are smaller publishing houses out there that will take submissions directly from an author. They function along broadly similar lines to the larger publishing houses but tend to be overlooked by most agents, meaning they can be a good route for a debut author to try especially if that publishing house is newer and looking to grow their list. But beware: Any publisher who expects the author to pay for everything is one to be avoided. This is known as vanity publishing, Scams and how to avoid them will be covered shortly, but when in doubt remember the Golden Rule: Publishers pay you; you do not pay publishers. Search engines will tell you a lot more than I know about vanity publishing which is basically a scam. Scams and avoiding them will be covered next.

Self/Independent Publishing

If you really want to release your book into the world then this is the route you are going to have to take, and in recent years Self-Publishing has become just as lucrative as traditional – not to mention popular. There are several different types of Self/Independent Publishing, but they all have one thing in common; you as an author are the project manager and the timeframe is in your hands.

Now, anyone who wants to publish a book can publish one – though this sometimes means self-published titles come with a certain stigma, namely that their quality may be lacking in comparison with traditionally published books. This is mainly because only stringently 'chosen' books are trad-published and therefore they are perceived to be better, having passed some kind of quality test. But again, books and their quality is entirely subjective and from the many self-published books I have read and reviewed I can happily say there are plenty of them which were better than trad-published ones, in terms of editing quality and story content.

As you are the project manager the quality of your work falls entirely on your shoulders; it is solely the author's responsibility to deliver a book that has the highest quality. This has nothing to do with your actual story, but the book as a product.

If you were to buy any product online, you would expect it to appear and function as advertised while also being safe. Books of course are a little different, but no less time should be spent on ensuring they are up to a certain standard. All books, no matter how they are published, must:

Be edited, formatted, proofread and free of all errors or as free of errors as is reasonable; one or two will always slip through, and this occurs in traditionally-published books at least as often as in self-published ones;

Have an attractive, eye catching cover;

This is what I like to call the Basic Anatomy of a book – we'll cover more of it in detail further ahead.

Because you are entirely in charge of the project this means you can employ as much or as little help to deliver a quality standard product. The age of the Internet has brought many of us closer not only as individuals, but also to products and services, several of which are relevant to self/indie publishing. In my case, which is more specifically laid out later on via the publishing road map, I wanted someone to edit my book, format it and upload it to Amazon*. I also needed someone to put together an attractive, eye-catching cover.

Everything I wanted above can be done yourself, if you are on a tight budget and are savvy with the tech side of things. However, my advice would be to employ the services of an editor at the very minimum and a cover artist. As with writing itself, everything else can be mastered via the many tutorials and guides throughout the virtual world.

Pricing and Budget

From experience it is highly recommended that anyone looking to self-publish invests in the services of both an editor and cover artist.

Depending on length of a book you should expect to budget for around £1000 to get this done well. Longer books may require more as they will take more time to edit professionally. This may sound like a lot, but it is a worthwhile, one-off investment to deliver the best possible product.

In conclusion, if you choose to pursue the route of self/indie publishing:
- You are the project manager.
- Your project needs to be edited and proofread/free of all errors as is reasonable.

- And have an attractive, eye catching cover.
- Expect to spend around £1000 or more depending on length.

While these are the necessities towards writing and then publishing, Book Production and Book Marketing is where the real journey begins.

* There are other self-publishing platforms but my advice would be to stick with Amazon and pursue others later.

Avoiding Scams

When anyone ventures into the unknown territory of publishing they can be naïve to the potential threat of scams that exist and believe me, they exist. Once upon a time I was one of those people, so I've opted to address scams here because I consider spotting and avoiding them an entry level lesson in the online publishing world.

Writers who are pursuing their dream are unfortunately open to those who are looking to take financial advantage of that. Although my advice is broad, it's important to research anyone who approaches you with an offer that may seem too good to be true. From offering book reviews to even fully publishing your work, what these potential scammers have in common is their attempt to make financial gain at your expense – a starry eyed author with big dreams and some hard-earned savings for a book project.

Not everyone falls under this category but someone who approaches you offering a service for a fee is a red flag. This can also work the other way too – when looking for any type of service online research is key. This isn't just advice for beginners but across the board. That research into who approached you and where they came from is vital. In the past I have blogged about potential review scams and other less than reputable services that resulted in many fellow authors avoiding such. Just a quick Google search might bring up more information on someone who has approached you, but if not you should treat the lack of information as a red flag. It may be that they are a reputable service just starting out but if you cannot find any information that's another red flag – a leap of faith may be required here, but the more red flags you identify the higher chance someone is trying to scam you.

You'll be surprised how special a potential scammer will attempt to make you feel, but remember to keep your feet on the ground, and if it involves any type of price and sounds slightly too good to be true, it's potentially a scam.

Managing Time

Time has already been mentioned and it will be more because the factor of time sits above near enough everything. From the trio to every other major factor that has led me to any success, all of it was and is governed by my own management of time.

Like writing, time management is something you have to find on an individual level and life will always do its best to get in the way. Through my passion for writing and wanting to get better, I adapted around life to answer to that. If you really want this then you'll find time and you'll treat time with value because that's exactly what I do. To me, it has always been a case of prioritising and even sacrificing other activities for writing.

It might be easy for me to tell you to make time but if you gradually add writing to your daily routine, even for a small amount of time, eventually it will start to feel like second nature or even a calling. Those few minutes a day turn to hours over weeks and without realising years have gone by all because you are answering to your calling.

Treat writing seriously over time and eventually it will treat you the same. This also goes for blogging and a social media presence. Generally, the more time you put in, eventually the more you will get out. It's a case of getting your mind and body used to the time you are spending with writing.

But how do I really manage my time?

To me, routine and gradual goal setting fosters time management.

For many years I've made writing my evening task. Some get up early to write first thing while I like to spend the day looking forward to it. This motivates me throughout the day and also means by the evening most of my chores and tasks are done so all I have left is writing. Over that time I've woven this routine into my life and have become used to it, so when I don't write, I feel as if I'm missing out.

As a rule, and even now when I'm writing I remove all distractions and disconnect myself from the world by placing myself in a quiet room alone. No phones, no television and even my laptop I'll disconnect from the internet. My desk is away from the window so all I can focus on is the writing. I tend to take regular breaks and because I'm a fidget I don't spend too long sat down. Setting a small writing goal for each time I'm sat down keeps me on track.

During the majority of 2020 I found that I had even more time than usual and so I made use of it to gradually increase my social media presence and write more blog posts. As 2021 started, my social media following became more engaged and resulted in an even larger following all because I put more time into it.

Book Production

> *"Write the book you want to write and don't try to anticipate the market. By the time your book is written, the zeitgeist will have already left you behind."*
>
> — Karl Relf,
> author of the DCI Brookes Series.

Book Production: The Modern Wonder of Publishing

THE INTERNET AGE HAS turned publishing into a much wider, less closed-doors environment, because now anyone can do it. This is both good and bad, depending on your personal stance. Only a few years ago it was extremely difficult to find a publisher or even self-publish without huge printing costs, and then there was the issue of having to store your stock of physical books before potentially finding vendors to sell them.

Amazon has cut all of that out and continue to revolutionise the way the industry functions. Their self-publishing program, Kindle Direct Publishing, is a huge outlet for modern book production. KDP now also includes their print-on-demand (POD) service which is both efficient and lucrative for the independent author.

POD means that authors no longer need to hold stock of their works. It also means Amazon doesn't either. It's farewell to propping doors open with full boxes of books or using them to level a table or two, because every time a reader orders a copy of your book, it is then printed and shipped to order – that is if your country/territory is covered by it. As long as your book fits within the templates and sizes they can print, this is a no-brainer that I recommend all authors use for their paperbacks.

Ebooks however, are slowly but surely taking their share of the market and I am both a supporter of and believer in digital publishing. It is my prediction that the digital market will only grow stronger. Most of the books I read are digital; it saves physical space and they are available straight away. With the focus of reducing our carbon footprint in the years to come, it's worth considering buying digital for your next read. To begin with, this book was exclusively digital to support that belief.

Most of my sales over the years have come from digital copies. Although some will argue that nothing beats that feeling of holding a book in your hands – and of course this is especially so for your own title, not to mention that 'book smell' but the world is moving closer and closer to fully digital. Embrace it.

Amazon also offers an exclusive distribution service for digital books known as Kindle Unlimited, a membership-based subscription for readers who can 'borrow' the e-version of your book for free. Royalties are earned from a set pot of money allocated by Amazon and they reward authors based on the number of page 'turns' registered per book. This can be quite lucrative for an author with numerous titles and a large readership, although if your book is enrolled in KU it must be exclusive to Amazon.

Kindle Unlimited also allows authors the option of setting the price of an ebook to 'free' for a limited number of dates over a set period of time, which is effective for promotion. All my works of fiction are currently enrolled in KU.

Book Production: The Basic Anatomy of a Book

JUST WHAT SHOULD THAT masterpiece of your look like in order to give it the best possible chance of selling? The Basic Anatomy of a book should contain these main attributes.

An Attractive Cover

Although mentioned previously in the Publishing Overview, I will reassert that having an attractive, eye-catching cover is possibly the most important and easiest way to sell your work. No matter what the consensus is, people **do** judge a book by its cover so having an attractive, professional-looking one is a must.

There are a host of trustworthy cost-effective graphic design service providers out there who can do some truly wonderful things with book covers. And trust me, this will give you the best possible chance of selling. Many readers have bought my books based solely upon the cover.

A Gripping Title

There are many theories around creating book titles, including the suggestion that they should be similar to those of recent best-sellers, but I've never bought into trying to emulate the titles of others. Make your book title unique, memorable and reflective of what the story is. Do your research, check to see if there are other titles like yours. There are thousands of words out there with combinations never used before.

The concept of naming my first book *Open Evening* was both literal and an opportunity to be unique. An Open Evening in the UK is similar to an Open House in the US, except it's based at a high school where prospective students visit and take a look around. The story is set during an 'Open Evening' so it felt natural to name it that. Plus as far as I am aware there are no books which share the same title.

When I titled *Darke Blood*, a vampire thriller, I tried to put it in line with that theme, and the word 'Darke' is both a play on words with the book's setting of 'Darke Heath', as well as the shadows to come. Of course, the word 'Blood' makes it a little more obvious vampires are involved. Most of my titles are literal and literal works well, but try to be unique and different.

An Enticing Blurb

Blurbs are supposed to give readers a teasing indication of where your book will take them. I normally leave blurb writing to the very end of the book production, or when the cover artist asks for one. Sometimes they can feel like a chore, but they are necessary and should relay enough information to entice a reader to pick up your story. They tie in with the importance of a book cover because they fill most of the space on the back of one.

As a rule I tend to keep my blurbs short and sharp. My method is to start off with a powerful quote that embodies the story, two or three paragraphs that set the scene and suggest where the story will go, followed by another quote to sign off.

For fiction, main characters and the conflict they aim to resolve makes for a good subject to put in the blurb along with mentioning the antagonist if there is one. Is the setting unique or worth noting? What makes this story stand out from anyone else's? What do you want readers to feel? What is at stake? I'm asking you these questions because someone else will, one day. If you have a good cover artist, they may also ask questions like this to get a grasp of what the cover should look like.

Blurb writing, much like book writing, comes from within and can be grasped from feeling the story. It's an exercise in summing up your work in a way that attracts readers.

Be Professionally Edited

The book may look good on the surface but within is where you'll find its true quality. This will only show if it has been edited by yourself and then a professional. An edited manuscript is just as vital as any of the above attributes and, to me, all four of them go hand in hand. I take editing so seriously I have dedicated the next page to it.

To conclude, the Basic Anatomy of a book should have the following:
- An attractive cover.
- A gripping title.
- An enticing blurb.
- Professional editing.

Book Production: Get Yourself an Editor

ONE OF THE BEST ways an author can grow and hone their craft is to have someone keep their work in check every now and then. Having your words assessed and edited by a professional is hugely important and just as vital as any attractive book cover will ever be.

Not only do editors steer an author in the right direction, but they can also help shape a story. Their job is to be a second set of eyes that not only correct any errors in your work, but also act as a rational, grounded advisor to make a book the best it can possibly be.

If you are serious about publishing then you will need to have that work of yours looked at by an editing professional. Whether it be for structure, spelling, grammar, or anything else, at least one set of eyes that isn't yours must grace that work before publishing.

There are so many reputable, hardworking editors to be found online, where many authors can vouch for their work. This will be a leap of faith in some senses but a good leap in the right direction if you research and find a good candidate.

At first, the concept of hiring an editor may seem quite daunting and when you first receive that edited manuscript back, you will feel partially violated and that's okay. In my case, when I first reached out to my wonderful editor Nicky with *Open Evening*, she returned my edited manuscript laced in coloured words. At the time I didn't really know what to expect but over time I have learned a good editor will clearly lay out what work they have done and any amendments they intend to make on your work.

In my case there were four different colours on that manuscript: one for corrections; one for delete; the rare but untouched black; and any advisory notes in green. It may have been a little jarring, but after so many books this is now our process.

Most editors are writers too and so they will do their work in that light. It's okay to disagree with anything they change as long as you can professionally and rationally explain it – this is your work after all and editors make changes with the best of intentions. Much of the time they go unnoticed as their work tends to blend with the writing style of that author. They will also be fluid with anything you question; it's your project after all.

A standard rule of thumb with editors and how they operate is to firstly receive a quote, pay half of it to secure the work while paying the second half on delivery. Some editors may even edit a sample amount of your work just to see if you like their style.

Book Marketing Basics: A Memoir and Roadmap

"Writing is an art form and you know your story better than anyone, so don't let people force their own 'rules' on you."

– Brooklynn Dean,
author of Amethyst and The Word of the Rock God.

Book Marketing Basics: The Truth and a Memoir

THE ADVICE I HAVE for marketing books – your creation, your labour of words, your book children or whatever you call them – starts with the most important statement in this whole book when it comes to that subject:

The best way to sell a book is to write another one, then another and then more.

That might sound like a cliché and you may have heard or read that advice elsewhere, but I cannot stress enough how important it is as an author to continually create and release new work. No book likes to be alone on the shelf, trust me. Content is king in the digital world and if you are serious about having your work read and seen in that world you need to produce it, consistently. To do this you'll need to be creative. This backs up the three words that are on the front of this book's cover. It also comes from experience.

It is my opinion that someone who has only written and released one book is not a true writer…

Whoa, steady on there. Before you put this book down in disgust, let me explain. You will probably agree that is a bold statement and it may sound controversial, but it's not intended to be. It's also just one part of a wider statement.

The reason I have focused on just this part is because my own journey to success only really began after I had published multiple titles.

Those who have written and released one book should not be overlooked for their work – writing a book is an exceptional achievement – but it is my opinion that someone who has only written and released one book is not a true writer, because anyone can write one book. But if that experience did not put them off doing it again, then they are a writer in my eyes.

Basically, if you are willing to go through all of that again – the process, the hours of work, the editing, the days and nights in eternal struggle to put those words into an orderly fashion, the shouting into an empty void – then you, my friend, are a writer. Truly.

And those with just the one book published or currently being written, you are already halfway there. Keep going. You want this, I want this, I want you to want this. Otherwise you wouldn't be reading this and I wouldn't have written it…

Many good honest people will say everyone has got a story in them and I would agree but a true writer has more than one story in them and it's up to that individual to find that story. Sometimes you'll have to dig deep and I was on my journey of writing my second book when I became, when I found myself as a writer – more on that soon.

Today, I stand with a backlist of books to my name. That sell regularly. But if it wasn't for that list then none of them would have sold because if you can convince one person to read your book, and if it means something to them, that reader will be inclined to at least know if you have other titles available. Having more titles available is an opportunity.

Not only does it appear that you are dedicated to writing but having those titles also carries a level of brand credibility and so that rolls nicely into my story…

A Memoir of Writing Destiny

This concept is indeed no revelation, but it is worth exploring further. Many of you can relate when it comes to your favourite author. Let's go back to 2005 when I was sixteen years old and stood without a clue about the real world or who I really wanted to be. The dream of being a writer was still forming within and back then the prospect of being anything and nothing all at once fed the imagination of the dreamer in me. Living near Heathrow Airport, and having grown up against the backdrop of planes constantly taking off over the fields opposite my home, it seemed that I was destined to eventually find a job there. That first job of cleaning those same airplanes didn't last anywhere near as long as the influence from what I found during one fateful shift. It happened to be a partly-weathered book and just then I didn't realise it would be my destiny. This dishevelled text was just sitting there, abandoned and headed for the trash. Even back then I knew you should never throw away a book but anything other than in flight magazines and pillows were deemed trash by the cleaning company. I took exception to that rule and kept this book – known as *Timeline* written by the well-known author, Michael Crichton.

I devoured that book from cover to cover in less than a week. The story whisked me away to medieval France by the vessel of realistic time travel through the science of quantum mechanics. This part-history, part-rescue action tale engrossed me. The reading experience still stands as one of my most immersive. This was my fiction awakening and it brought a desire to explore more of Crichton's books.

Today on my shelves there are more of his books than any other author. Why? Because as soon as I got done reading *Timeline* I bought another title by him because they were available, and that next reading experience hooked me in even further. Then I bought another and another until his works began to inspire my own journey in writing. That journey was partly possible because of Crichton's back list.

Some years later I learned of his passing, which carried the final, sad feeling that I would never be able to thank him for those stories and for inadvertently handing me my own destiny. Of course, the person who left that book behind also takes some responsibility, whoever you are, thank you. Destiny can fall into our hands during the most unexpected of moments.

The inspiration Crichton had on my work will never be known to him. If you ever have an opportunity to thank an artist for their influence on you, then do it. This will mean probably more than anything to them.

The lesson: Having a back list will increase your chances of sales. And it is imperative you work towards releasing more books on a consistent basis.

As an author I am always planning or looking towards a new project on the horizon. If you were to ask me what I planned on writing next I could give you at least three different projects. I'm either editing, drafting or preparing a project for release. And if someone takes an interest in your work and does ask you what's next, it sounds like you know what you're doing… more importantly and to me, I write because I love it. Some moments in life are just destiny and finding a book galvanised mine.

Book Marketing Basics: Do the Work: A Roadmap to Consistent Content

I SHOULD PROBABLY BACK up the previous section with explaining how I released six books in five years. This can benefit you if I share the important details of my own journey just to show you how I did it.

Although I have mentioned it before, I will say again that it is imperative to plan and manage expectations, and I did to an extent – circumstances were continually changing during the five years and so did my plans. This isn't a great advert for planning, but sometimes you just need to roll with the punches. What remained was my ambition to release as much work in different genres and lengths as possible. As a reader myself I want variety and as a writer it is my firm belief that if you can write a book, the genre is variable. My deeper reasonings will unfold as the journey is broken down below. This is without mentioning goings on in the background known as life – those punches I had to roll with came from snowstorms, heatwaves and even house moves. Life will get in the way sometimes and it's up to you as a writer to find a way to carry on through whatever it throws you.

Context

By 2015 my writing endeavours consisted of zero works published along with zero results in getting a literary agent, but there were positives; there always are. The most important one was that the science fiction series I wrote and completed served as quite a wonderful lesson in how to write while also managing expectations, which awoke me from the starry-eyed dream that just wasn't going to happen.

In the three years previous I had learnt to write by spending up to four hours a night pecking away at the keyboard. This was usually on top of a full day at work, and it was hard work but it resulted in three completed books (and one dead laptop keyboard). This time ended up becoming the most important of my writing career and, through sometimes painful trial and error I learned a lot about my own capabilities as an author. To this day I have no formal qualifications in writing, just thousands of hours experience writing stories through hard work alone, and trust me, there is no substitute for hard work. This of course, isn't to impugn anyone who has studied the English language, it is my long-term ambition to one day do the same.

It was also in this year (2015) that I decided to drop the science fiction project and start fresh. Starting again was not only liberating creatively but now my imagination was free, no longer bogged down by one project and series. For those who are considering writing a series, the value of exploring other projects between books will serve as both a palate-cleanser and aid your growth as a creator. We must always look to expand beyond our original means to exploit our growth fully.

My decision stood between penning a superhero comedy with no source material or a fast-paced horror inspired by my own school days (that just happened to have some source material from my mid-teen writings I'd kept in a box gathering dust). Using one short story that originally consisted of six lined A4 pages made up of mostly scratchy writing, I managed to fashion that along with my own experiences into *Open Evening*.

And before you ask, yes, my high school days were *that* bad. Even before the monsters jumped out of the shadows, most of the story is inspired by how bad that school was. Writing a book that combined both served as therapy and a middle finger up to those days while also serving as more therapy. Yes, that bad...

Next came the prospect of self-publishing, which had been at my forefront for a while. During the few years I'd spent on social media I'd built up some contacts, one of which included a small independent publisher to whom I reached out to. Not only would she edit, but format and publish *Open Evening* on my behalf and then all I would need to do is find a cover artist. I would have full control of royalties and the material thereafter. This type of publishing is somewhere between self-publishing and independent publishing, hence why I consider them the same.

It didn't take long to draft and then edit *Open Evening*. This liberation of the imagination and part therapy worked wonders, so in late 2015 Satin Publishing agreed to take on *Open Evening* – Satin Publishing is an independent editing, formatting and publishing company run by Nicky Fitzmaurice, and has now worked on several of my books, as well as those of many others whose works have been brought to publication. This is where my road to publishing began and we agreed to bring *Open Evening* to the world in September 2016. This allowed me plenty of time to not only edit the book thoroughly, but also to draft another book because early on my vision was to consistently produce content.

The Roadmap

The journey I took to get five books published in six years was a winding road of doing the work on one book while planning the next few in hand. **Time** was firmly on my side to begin with. I was determined to create as many books as I could, not only to show what I could do, but also because I enjoyed it and I wanted to get better at it. I am equally as determined now, but as you can see in the timeline below, in the latter stages my blogging endeavours began to play a more important role. The years are measured from September 2015 onwards.

Year 1

- **2015: Drafted and edited Book 1 *Open Evening*** – Reached out to Nicky of Satin Publishing and agreed a publication date for the next year; September 2016.

- **Early 2016: Began to draft my second novel *Darke Blood*.**

More Context

To this day *Darke Blood* served was the most difficult project I have ever endured. I had to dig deep to complete this story, in a time when I was still finding myself as an author. The wonderful thing is, I did find myself in that way while writing this project. I had no source material other than an idea to do a story about vampires. If you can fashion a story out of just a couple of ideas I would say you are a writer, and that struggle is represented by arguably my best ever book although that is something I leave up to everyone else. The reason I mention *Darke Blood* in this fashion is because during the drafting process it became clear that the only way the story was going to work was by connecting it to the same world as *Open Evening* and so the beginnings of a wider series were formed pretty much on the fly.

Back to the Roadmap

- **Summer 2016:**

    Drafted Book 2: *Darke Blood* with realisation it is set in the same world as *Open Evening*.

    Edited Book 1: *Open Evening* **for the second** time and included references to *Darke Blood* to plant eventual series idea. Then sent Book 1 manuscript to editor Nicky.

    Received the edited *Open Evening* **manuscript back** and agreed any potential changes. The book was then ready to be launched after Design For Writers put together a fantastic cover.

Preliminary work then began on Book 3: *Cemetery House.* This is the sequel to *Open Evening* even though I am unsure how the first book will be received – ideas were beginning to flow for the series.

- **September 2016: Book 1 *Open Evening* is launched.** It finds moderate success in the Amazon UK Occult Paperback Charts peaking at #2. Close friends and family leave some all-important initial reviews and even some folks I haven't heard from in a while buy a copy.

Year 2

- **Winter 2016: Organisation begins for the publication of Book 2 *Darke Blood.*** Release will be in May of 2017, just 8 months after the release of *Open Evening*. Both Nicky and Design for Writers are available and booked.

- **Early 2017: Book 2 *Darke Blood* is edited by me and then sent to professional editor Nicky.** It returns with some changes which are agreed along with advice to change the ending from a quick wrap up to something more drawn out – this is one of the many reasons you need an editor.

- **Design for Writers put together yet another beautiful cover for *Darke Blood*.**

- **May 2017: *Darke Blood* is launched.** It has some success but not as much as *Open Evening*. At this moment I decide my next release will be a stand-alone superhero comedy I first envisioned back in 2015.

- **Summer 2017: Full drafting begins on book 3 *Cemetery House*,** the sequel to *Open Evening* also sharing the same world as *Darke Blood*. I'm determined to make this series a success and so I go full steam ahead.

- **Drafting of Book 3 *Cemetery House* is completed** and I take a two-week holiday to France. There is wine and cheese and sunshine.

- **Autumn 2017: Return home and immediately begin drafting that superhero comedy *The Teleporter*.** Now it has spent some time growing in my imagination it doesn't take long to draft and I decide to make this Book 3. My reasoning for this is Book 1 and Book 2 are still growing a readership so releasing another book in that series is too soon. Let's do a standalone instead.

Year 3

- **Late 2017: A master plan is put into place for 2018:** That being the release of two books in one year. Standalone Book 3 *The Teleporter* and Book 4 *Cemetery House* the sequel to Book 1 and so establishing the *Order of the Following* series.

- **Early 2018: Drafting begins on the next book in the *Order of the Following* series *Darke Awakening*,** my fifth book.

- **Late winter to early Spring 2028: Book 3 *The Teleporter* is edited by Nicky.** Some changes are made – the ending now has a better flow. Design for Writers put together another fantastic cover.

- **Book 3 *The Teleporter* is published in early May 2018 to similar results as Book 2.** Okay but not great. The machine continues.

- **Summer 2018**: Drafting of book 5 *Darke Awakening* is complete. Editing begins for Book 4, *Cemetery House,* due out later in 2018.

- **Summer/Autumn 2018: Book 4 *Cemetery House* is sent to editor Nicky. Design for Writers put together the awesome cover.**

- **Autumn/Winter 2018: Book 4 *Cemetery House* is eventually published**. After some technical hitches via Amazon the release date was missed for the paperback edition, though the ebook version arrived on schedule. Sales are the lowest of any release so far. It's been a tough year, and just a month after this release I am set to move house – stress levels are high and so Book 5 *Darke Awak-*

ening is shelved with no proposed release date. I feel lost.

Year 4

- **Winter 2018:** Stress levels eventually simmer down and I manage to work through my roughest time in writing. A lot of lessons are learned. Perhaps there wasn't much demand for a sequel to my debut along with the missed release date? Either way I eventually work through the disappointment and decide to start again on a standalone writing project to find myself. At this point my blogging/social media following begins to rise faster than normal. That 'wave' is coming in and my presence is being noticed.

- **Winter 2018:** In order to find myself and my writing again I opt to hand write this new project in its entirety. This eventually becomes Book 5 *The Ghost Beside Me*, a paranormal romance short story. I don't envision publishing anytime soon as moving into my new place takes priority. Blogging numbers are steadily rising towards the end of the year and then I take a break from social media for a month. The move into my new place is a success.

- **Winter 2018:** The year ends. It's been one of my busiest in and out of writing. Twitter engagement and follows begin to rise as I set my sights of blogging more to take advantage of rising numbers and this 'wave'.

- **2019:** A pinnacle year for my Hall of Information blog which is nominated four times for different awards. Still the numbers rise and I continually produce content for a growing following. Now that I have four books available, I spend some time promoting them throughout the year, *Darke Blood* is downloaded 3000 times during one of these free promos.

- **Summer 2019:** After spending much of the year focusing on blogging, I look towards releasing Book 5 *The Ghost Beside Me*. This book is dedicated to my late grandfather since it is inspired by a ghost story he once shared with me. The handwritten project is converted into a 60-page novella/short story.

Year 5

- **Autumn 2019:** I choose to fully self-publish Book 5 as it's quite short, so I just ask Design for Writers to create a cover. Everything else – formatting, editing and publishing – I take on myself after reaching out to a few bloggers to read advance copies.

- **Winter 2019: Book 5 *The Ghost Beside Me* is published**. After an extremely successful year of blogging and social media engagement this release is my second most successful after Book 1. The re-views for *The Ghost Beside Me* quickly accumulate, with more posted in six months than any of my other books managed in a similar timeframe.

- **Early 2020:** With *Darke Blood* being downloaded 3000 times just some months previous, I decide to continue with the *Order of the Following* series. *Darke Awakening* is already drafted and so I organise publication with Nicky and ask Design for Writers to make a cover. I edit and revisit the story – this is while my blogging and social media engagement continues to rise.

- **Spring 2020: Book 6 *Darke Awakening* is edited and then sent to Nicky with a proposed September release.** Drafting immediately begins on the last book in the series, Book 7 *Darke Apocalypse,* which is not inspired by the events of 2020.

- **Summer 2020: Book 7 *Darke Apocalypse* is drafted.** Now my main focus turns to blogging as I celebrate six years since the launch of my Hall of Information. At this point more and more authors/bloggers are noticing my content and I decide to write this book.

- **Summer 2020: Drafting begins for *Consistent Creative Content* which soon becomes Book 7. The dream continues.**

- **Autumn 2020: Book 6 *Darke Awakening* is released to moderate success.** The e-version being available for pre-order – an option I had never explored before. Several pre-orders ensured the release was a success, along with handful of paperback sales. This caps off the greatest month ever (September 2020) for paid sales, with every book in my backlist being sold over that time. Things are starting to pay off and I know more now about book promotion and publishing than ever before.

- **Early 2021:** Things go from strength to strength in both blogging and authoring. By mid-February *The Teleporter* reaches #1 and becomes an Amazon Best Seller after a once in a lifetime featured deal via BookBub. Reviews pour in for the book while more and more readers are tuning into my Hall of Information Blog. Twitter engagement increases by the month with a following that grows from five thousand to nearly ten thousand in under six months. It took some years but a potential career in writing for me looks possible in my lifetime.

Partial Debrief

Let's take a moment and put aside the many details I've included in the roadmap for now.

Time was and still is the biggest factor in what governed the publishing of six books in five years. From the start I gave myself a year in hand between finishing the draft of Book 1 to publishing it. That rolling time gap allowed me to manage each book release and spend time on what was next.

This year in hand method means whatever project I am drafting currently *should* go on sale a year later. Along with the availability of both my editor and cover artist, time management played a key part in the whole operation. As the number of projects increased so did my working relationship with the wider publishing team. Both my editor and cover artist were happy to take on each project.

In conclusion, there were highs, lows and many different struggles – some of which we will discuss further ahead. Doing the work and writing these books was important to me and that is the moral to all of this.

If you really want it, go and get it.

The Highs, Lows and Many Different Struggles: Was it worth it?

MUCH LIKE I MENTIONED at the very beginning of this book, all of this is in the eye of the beholder. Now I have shared my book writing journey, it's important to draw my own conclusions and reflections with a hope that you, as a reader, can relate to them. If you can go just a step further and take something from this, then I will have succeeded.

The truth is, for as long as I could remember I have wanted to be a storyteller. It has been my dream to be an author, specifically, since I was immersed into the world of reading. That engrossing, floating feeling where you forget the outside world and are totally among the words – this is a feeling I've only known a handful of times (*Timeline* comes to mind) and it is also the feeling I have chased in telling stories. From the road map you can tell my priority above all was to tell stories passionately and to constantly improve while doing so. My imagination deserves the absolute best I could do to showcase it.

From the very start of Book 1, I fell in love with the concept of creating, and so working on that book galvanised it. Everything about my writing endeavours that followed is irrespective of sales, reviews and any kind of following I've built. I appreciate all those things but, above all else, I write because I enjoy it. Everything else is a resultant of that pure raw passion. Now I look back at those books and the stories inside them with nothing but affection. The true lesson here; **do it for you**.

The road of life is long and so is the one of a storyteller. There will be times of struggle and it's important to manage your expectations constantly. On reflection, choosing to publish two books in 2018 was the absolute limit of my capabilities. I know that now because I did it and learned a lot. Although it was a stretch, along with it being the same year to get myself on the property ladder and literally do more paperwork than I had ever done, it was worthwhile. By 2017 I had two books published. by the end of the next year it had doubled to four and that was when my social media numbers began to rise.

It wasn't all good news because by the time Book 4 went live, my mental health was in tatters. Expectations, external goings on and all-around other problems took their toll. As I said life will go on inside and outside of the words. That book release was not as great as envisioned, sales were low and the realisation came that perhaps all the good people who supported Book 1 didn't fancy a sequel or didn't even know about it. Happily, Book 4 has since picked up several ratings and sold very well – though I know my books aren't to everyone's taste. If you want to know the real moral to all of this, it is that your writing should only aim to please one person, yourself. Everything else after reaching the end doesn't actually matter, but the words do, so do it for you.

It didn't take long for me to pull myself out of what was just a short phase of half exhaustion and half expectations getting out of hand. It's okay to be down about things and I'd poured every emotion I know into these books. If you ever want to truly know who I am, read my books. I also had a wonderful friendship group at the time and still do. My other half is, and probably always will be, the source of the stability I need to write more than just moody poetry although that is no disrespect to any form of poetry.

What followed after Book 4 was a semi-absence from publishing new material. Resting is important for both the mind and body. My advice with this is to take as long as you need to repair yourself. Practice self-care and do everything you can to protect that mind of yours; it's the only one you have. You know your physical and mental limitations. This modern world of busy-ness can take its toll on our mental health and that's something we all have a duty of care with; not just our own but those around us.

If my writing efforts were slowing down, by 2019 my blogging endeavours were quickly picking up. Having a backlist and my blog content created a combination that caused the number of views to skyrocket. We are moving closer to how I got those numbers first mentioned at the start. They coincide with everything I've covered so far. After some years of blogging and publishing, it was finally starting to become worthwhile, the words were becoming my calling.

From what began as journey mainly for me became something both unexpected and wonderful, So I'll say the whole thing was worthwhile. But this story is only half complete.

Book Marketing: Selling and Promotion

"My advice is to persevere. If you're disillusioned and need a break, that's fine. Take a long break if you need to, but try again someday, because writers who persevere are most likely to succeed in the end. It's also worth knowing that it's easier to achieve publication success in niche markets because there is less competition in specialist sectors."

— Susie Kearley,
freelance journalist and author of Pestilence.

Book Marketing: The Art of Indirect Selling for Authors and Bloggers

I'LL ADMIT, INCLUDING AN autobiographical roadmap into the Book Marketing section may be a stretch, but it's all for the cause in helping fellow wordsmiths. Context is the key for me in delivering this to you; a hopefully an engaged reader who is looking to learn something. The only way I can guide you is by relaying what I did. Building from my best advice of writing more and more books, just what else can you do on social media and beyond to sell your books?

The process of selling books, like all products, will involve methods of marketing. But first it's time yet again to refer to another vital attribute outside the trio.

Selling anything in this world is simply exploiting a perceived lack of or need for something, and that is the sense you must create if you want to sell a book, get any kind of social media engagement, or pick up blogging views.

There are plenty of high-level salespeople who, over the years, have created a false sense of urgency in order to pressure folks into buying something. You don't need to do that. I've never done that, nor have I ever exploited anyone, but the whole philosophy of success does revolve around creating a sense of need and urgency for people to engage with you on social media.

My philosophy is you don't have to convince people to buy your book, you have to convince them to buy into you. And then they will eventually buy your work.

Unfortunately, just throwing books at people doesn't sell them most of the time. There are no shortcuts to selling quick. But I do know how to convince people, one at time in some senses, to believe in you even though for a while I didn't even know I was doing it.

So just how do you convince people to buy into you?

By being relatable, professional, supportive, genuine, honest and decent through all of your endeavours as a writer or blogger online.

This is something you cannot fabricate; if you try, you *will* get found out. And everyone is drawn to decency eventually. It's also something that cannot be achieved quickly. This journey is a marathon, not a sprint… but it will be worthwhile. Although this advice is broad it's also a fantastic opportunity to be as creative as you like in all of your endeavours across social media.

This is what I call the 'art of indirect selling'. The focus isn't on selling anything; that's just a side effect of what you are really trying to achieve. And if people invest in you as a person, they will loyally follow you and support your book writing/blogging endeavours. This theory is derived through trust, and trust alone sells more products than anything. So if you have that backlist, and people invest in you through trust its theirs for the taking. And the biggest take away from this method, though, is the fun and satisfaction it will bring. This is also a social-heavy activity. If adopted well, you'll be meeting and connecting with likeminded folks from all over the world. Meeting new people is great, especially online because it's easy.

Using this philosophy, in 2018 my Hall of Information Blog turned a huge corner and that's something we will explore further on. My outlook on sales is more of a state of mind but there are also a range of physical Book Marketing and Promotion methods you can employ as opposed to just philosophical ones.

Book Marketing: Pricing

AT THIS STAGE YOU could possibly be looking to publish your first title or you may even have several already available. Money really isn't something you should expect to make straight away or at least for a while. Money is not why I do this but, in order to be positive, you must consider your published works as investments in yourself for the future.

With that in mind and because you want the best possible chance of your book selling, I suggest you aim relatively low in terms of pricing.

There are a bunch of standards that various folks from all walks of publishing will try to lecture you with, but we're going to keep it simple.

For an ebook, anything priced over my standard of $/£2.99 is probably too much and won't sell.

Exceptions:

An anthology that's longer than the 'standard' length of a book;

Works of non-fiction;

A book that is relatively short.

The price for the first two can be set higher than usual, while in the third instance, you would probably want to think about pricing it lower. There are different royalty rates depending on price. Amazon will be better at explaining these.

For a paperback and in my case using Amazon's print on demand service, your price will totally rely on how much it costs for Amazon to produce that book. If your book has a higher page count or is physically bigger in size this will affect that cost and then the price. So I'm going to be broad here and say roughly a 75,000 word book should be priced at £7 to £8.99 and perhaps a little more in US dollars (taking into account the currency exchange rate).

There are many variables to consider when deciding on price, but I price my shorter paperback works way lower. This is because I don't rely on the royalties financially, and the works are cheaper to produce.

Book Marketing: Promotion Basics

THE SALESMAN IN ME couldn't sell clouds to the sky, but that's okay because my books have been downloaded thousands of times all around the world. From the absolute novice to a seasoned veteran, all writers share the same struggle: the struggle of telling the world your work exists. It sometimes feels like nobody can hear us, when all we are trying to do is shout about our work, but there are several ways in which we can amplify our voices. Book Promotion is the way in which you can amplify your voice to get readers to hear you.

First, though, be prepared to know this:

> Selling books isn't easy;
>
> Selling books will most likely cost money;
>
> Selling books doesn't guarantee a review;
>
> Selling books doesn't guarantee the reader will like it;
>
> Selling books and your desperation to do so will be exploited if you aren't careful;
>
> Selling books takes time and requires patience;
>
> Selling books can be fun.

Your book, even if it fits within the Basic Anatomy guidelines and Pricing guidelines won't just sell itself, but it still has a good chance. Along with everything else covered up to this point, there are a range of ways to get that voice of yours amplified. The next sections will explore these Book Promotion methods in detail.

Book Marketing: Book Promotion Methods: Everyone Loves a Freebie

ONE OF THE BEST ways you can achieve maximum sales is to temporarily set your ebook price to free. Those who have published via Amazon KDP can arrange this by enrolling their title in Kindle Unlimited, which then allows you to set that title to free for a limited time during a certain period. As mentioned earlier, enrolling in KU allows authors to benefit from earning royalties through ebook page reads, though to do this it must be exclusive to Amazon.

There are routes to making a title permanently free, but I've always tried to make this type of promotion an occasion so that it builds some sort of urgency and has a level of exclusivity.

Although this technically doesn't count as a paid sale, it's still a transaction. This is a please all, target all, blanket approach to gaining a readership and is most probably the nearest to 100% guaranteed to get one or more downloads. It still doesn't guarantee the reader will read it or like it but that's the case in every book sale.

Many authors remain stubbornly against the concept of making their work free to read and refuse to do it. I'm very much in favour of it, because any type of distribution is good distribution and Amazon have separate charts for free titles which are a lot easier to climb, giving more visibility. If you want your book to be read, then this is a surefire method to make sure it is. In particular, this is a great way for beginner authors to build an initial readership and get a foothold in the market.

Strategy

Like everything else in this journey, your expectations must be managed. If your book has only a few reviews this may weigh upon the success of a free book promotion. Your social media following and reach will also have an influence – the more of a following you have, the better amount of downloads you are likely to get – although as the title of this section suggests, everyone loves a freebie. If you use the right hashtags and time things right, you can expect some downloads through your social media posts.

The time of year may also have a direct reflection on how successful the promotion is. Over time I have learned that books within the horror or thriller genres normally do quite well in the run up to Halloween as well as during the winter months, romance books can utilize the opportunity of Valentine's day, and the summer is perfect for a beach type read – in particular *The Teleporter* always sells well during the summer months. Generally, the weekend is better for social media reach as more people are online. Timing is everything in book promotion.

In order to create some sense of urgency that encourages maximum downloads, my strategy consists of making a book available for free only for a short period of time. Three days is enough, but less is even more effective and bolsters that sense of urgency. A combination of weekdays and weekend days are particularly effective. National holiday weekends are also great because a greater number of users will be online – this is especially so in the USA as they have numerous national holidays throughout the year and a high population.

Having a book available for free is only a partial step of Book Promotion and is even more effective when used in conjunction with other methods. Combining a free promotion with some advertising will amplify your voice and the chances of it being heard. Effective types of advertising are covered further ahead.

Advantages of a Free Book Promotion

Very effective and normally guarantees at least one download, but you can most probably expect more;

Easy to organise;

Free to do (if you don't use paid advertisements);

Amazon chart placement will temporarily improve, creating better visibility during that time if the book is downloaded enough. This wil bring even more pairs of new eyes to the book;

If the book is enrolled in Kindle Unlimited you can expect some royalties from page reads if the book is read by those with a membership to Kindle Unlimited after the promotion.

Disadvantages

Royalties from free downloads are zero;

If the book is relatively new and has only a few reviews it might not be downloaded by a lot of readers;

Many people will just grab a free book without thinking and then discover they don't like it. This may result in an influx of lower ratings.

Book Marketing: Book Promotion Methods: Mailing lists

Even with book sales it can be more about who you know as opposed to what you know. Having contacts is a power source to help drive books sales if used effectively. A mailing list is a great method of directly connecting to potential readers in an intimate, personable way and is highly effective in reaching those who might buy your work.

Contacts in all walks of life are built up over years and could be a mix of family, friends, work colleagues plus those you have networked with online. Most of them you will know in some way and that can be instrumental in convincing them to buy your work. To begin with you may not have a substantial list of email contacts, but this is something I recommend you work towards building.

Strategy

Considering the law when it comes to GDPR it is recommended you use a mailing list provider; many can be found online and offer free or paid services. At least this way if you are collecting many different email addresses the messages you send out will include an option to unsubscribe. It will also help you organise and keep track of your contacts all in one place.

Over the years I have collected many different contacts and their email addresses through blogging, authoring and even from close family and friends. Every so often I will send out a blanket newsletter that normally focuses on recent book release news or a promotion coming up. As a rule I don't send them out too regularly as I don't want to be perceived as a nuisance. If used effectively to communicate with contacts, mailing lists are a great way to sell books and keep in contact with readers.

Advantages of Mailing Lists

It's relatively easy to set up and send out a newsletter to a specific demographic;

Having the 'right' contacts will drive book sales;

Free if you don't choose a paid provider. Although most will charge you after reaching a certain number of contacts;

Great for organising your contacts all in one place;

A direct way to reach readers.

Disadvantages of Mailing Lists

Some contacts will most likely unsubscribe eventually;

Not everyone may read your newsletter;

Only really effective with a much larger following.

Book Marketing: Book Promotion Methods: Paid Advertising

When it comes to advertising for Book Promotion there are two main types; Paid Advertising and Free Advertising. This section is dedicated to the paid methods I have found the most effective.

Paid Advertising

Most of the time, paid advertising is the more effective way of amplifying your voice which in turn drives sales (in theory). It's also a nearly endless rabbit hole of variety. From many different websites to major social media platforms, there are a lot of places where you can advertise your book for money and normally the more you pay, the better reach you'll get. In order of overall effectiveness, here are the best and most effective paid advertising methods I've used over the years.

Book Promotion Websites (Paid)

Book Promotion websites are my go-to advertisers and have helped all my works reach new readers, and therefore higher chart positions along with accumulating reviews. But what exactly is a book promo site and how do they work? Most sites boast access to large followings, normally through mailing lists that they buy. Their website might have a high amount of traffic also. After you submit a book for consideration and pay them a fee, they will include an advertisement of your book in an email newsletter which is distributed to that following. Some will even feature the work on their website and mention it on their own social media channels.

High-end book promotion sites tend to have stricter submission guidelines and may even read the submitted title in its entirety before consideration. This is why it's important for a book to have a good basic anatomy. BookBub is a promotional site held in quite high regard and so it can be difficult to get an application accepted by them. But, as I mentioned before, they also promise 'good returns'.

Further ahead we will look into the results of various book promotions I have run over the years.

Strategy

As I mentioned, the strategy of using Book Promotion sites to advertise a free book is a highly effective way to amplify your voice and get an impressive number of downloads. Firstly, it's important to do some research and find out if the sites you plan to use are effective and reputable. Some authors like myself will publish their most recent book promotion endeavours in a blog post listing the sites used and detailing, which were effective. You can find a recent list of sites I've used via my blog's resources page.

When it comes to payment I highly recommend using a third-party payment provider such as PayPal. Most take PayPal and it can be a good indicator of whether or not a site is fully reputable. PayPal allows users to organise refunds if a service has not been fully received while also keeping your bank details separate. When paying for anything online, the more secure it is, the better.

With a little coordination combining paid advertising sites with a free book promotion is even more effective when using the multiple sites at once. Many sites will advertise free or even discounted books so there is plenty of choice out there.

An advanced strategy would be using some during a free promotion and then others when the book resumes to its normal or discounted price after – with the book's general profile improved by the free run, any paid sales right after should push the book up the paid sales chart.

Advantages of Book Promotion Sites (Paid)

Most paid book promo sites are affordable and easy to use/sign up to;

They have a wide reach for effective distribution/sales, which is continually growing;

Some higher end sites promise high sales/downloads;

Very effective when used correctly.

Disadvantages

You have to pay;

There's no guarantee that it will lead to sales;

Some sites do not carry out what they promised;

There will most likely be submission guidelines – minimum reviews, professional-looking cover, flexible dates;

Some sites don't always operate for particularly long, so up to date research is key to finding the best book promo sites.

Facebook Advertising

Although Facebook advertising is complex, it is a detailed way of reaching specific demographics who could potentially become your readership. I've had some success with Facebook over the years, mainly through trial and error, but never have I spent serious money.

Facebook's advertising interface allows the user to target pretty much anyone as broadly or specifically as desired. The consensus in effective advertising is to find someone who will like your specific niche by targeting them through interests, or other factors such as age, location, etc. This is exactly how Facebook advertising works and it can be powerful if used properly. While being broad may seem like the better way to reach a quantity of readers, it hardly seems to work on Facebook unless your product is very mainstream – wanting to be mainstream and actually being mainstream are two separate things and that's the wake up call you need before pouring money anywhere in advertising. Work on convincing the individual first, then work towards larger groups.

Setting up an advertisement on Facebook might seem quite daunting, but it's easy enough to use and near enough limitless when it comes to targeting demographics. Even for a small amount of money you can expect results which you can track in real time, so it's easy to know whether or not an ad campaign is working.

Strategy

In order to advertise on FB, you're going to need a page and preferably some followers along with some money. My initial journey into social media started with Facebook and my page's following; mostly family and friends at the time, this was my initial target audience, which I intended to build upon.

Very early on in this journey my core value was to convince readers to invest in me and my work on a personal level. Convincing a friend of a friend or friends of the family is much easier than approaching a complete stranger, as there is already some level of rapport between the two parties. This concept also reinvents the wheel that is word of mouth, but with the social media giant behind your efforts.

Facebook's advertising platform is able to cater to this particular strategy as you can directly target those who like your page and their friends. Over time my main strategy when it comes to Facebook ads is to keep it relatively local to your friendship circle and branch out through them.

Like most of this journey it's important to plan and set a realistic achievable goal. While world domination may appear possible through Facebook ads, it's more likely that won't happen no matter how much the platform will try to convince you otherwise.

After running plenty of ad campaigns over the years I have found Facebook most effective for:

1. Enhancing or boosting announcements;
2. Telling followers and their friends about current free book promotions.

Everything else, I'm yet to fully explore mainly because over these years Facebook has moved down my rankings in terms of social media platforms I am active on. Like the promotion methods mentioned before, I usually run a Facebook ad in conjunction with them.

Paying for Page Likes

In the earlier trial and error days I specifically ran Facebook ad campaigns to simply get more page likes. I found this seemed to be a quantity over quality result where most who liked the page during the campaign didn't engage afterward and therefore, it was not worth doing. There is such thing as the right engagement, and those blindly liking your page without reason isn't within that bracket.

> **Top Tip:** You can indirectly get more page likes through Facebook ads if you boost a post that targets new followers. If non-followers were to 'Like' that boosted post, you are then able to invite them to like your page. If they choose to do so this will most likely lead to an engaged following.

Advantages of Facebook Advertising

It's limitless in terms of targeting certain demographics so the potential reach is huge;

Relatively cheap and you are able to pause or stop campaigns in real time;

You can budget specifically to your spending limitations;

Relatively easy to use;

You can optionally choose to run an ad on Instagram at the same time.

Disadvantages

You have to pay;

Some ads may not run depending on the content of the post as they have to be approved by Facebook;

No guarantee it will lead to sales;

Demographics are limited to who is actually on Facebook.

Book Marketing: Book Promotion Methods: Free Advertising

WHILE PAYING FOR ADVERTISING may be effective, there are also some fantastic outside-the-box ways of amplifying your voice for nothing at all.

Book Promotion Websites (Free)

There are plenty of Book Promotion websites that will happily feature your work for free. Some paid sites offer a free option that is either first come, first serve or 'pot luck', while other sites just feature any title for free – normally in exchange for signing up to their mailing list at the very least. There are also others who offer the option of an 'honour' system, in which you pay whatever you think is fair. Also, like paid sites, in the ever-evolving world of the Internet they tend to come and go, so research is imperative.

Strategy

I've never used free Book Promotion websites as a sole way of promoting a book so it's hard to gauge how effective they really are. As with the the paid methods previously mentioned, I tend to use a handful of free sites to bolster my already paid advertising campaign for a free book.

Advantages of Free Book Promotion Websites
Free/easy to sign up.

Disadvantages
Most sites will only feature books that are free or discounted.

Giveaways

Technically, in order to give away a physical copy of your book, it will involve some cost which is to firstly order a copy and then sending it out but the act of running a giveaway is free on most platforms. Giveaways are an effective way to create a certain buzz around your social media presence and to get a wider interest in the work you are planning to give away.

Strategy

As mentioned before, everyone loves a freebie and the concept of giving a physical copy of your book away for free will attract interest. This interest may just be temporary but if you're like me, you'll take that, as opposed to zero interest…

Running a giveaway is fairly simple. You create a post on social media stating what is being given away (your book) followed by the entry details and basic rules. In the past I have created and linked a separate note or post which lists the full rules of entry. Some platforms have certain rules on giveaways so it's best to do some research. Pick the winner(s) either by random selection or your choice and then send them a copy of your book.

Typically, giving away a physical copy of your book will involve a level of cost, specifically those relating to ordering a copy or copies and sending it/them out. But you'll have to ship the book firstly to you (to sign) and then to the winner(s). To skip this extra cost in the past I have just shipped the book unsigned straight to the winners through Amazon. It's important to advertise what exactly the recipients will be receiving; for me it was an unsigned copy on that occasion.

Giveaways are a great way of creating buzz around a particular work or to celebrate milestones while also generating wider interest in your social media presence and wider works. Using multiple platforms is the best way to get any success from a giveaway and is also an indirect method to attract traffic from one to the other.

Remember: **everyone loves a freebie**, and predominantly I've run giveaways on my Facebook page and only those who are on Facebook can enter which means when advertised to my much larger Twitter following this indirectly gets more likes and engagement for the page. Those authors with money to spend can also benefit from using Facebook advertising to expand the reach of a giveaway post, but word of mouth is normally enough.

Advantages of Giveaways

It will most likely get a lot of interest in a short space of time;

It doesn't cost a lot, but this is dependent on the postage/price of ordering a copy of your work(s);

You can indirectly gain likes or follows by attracting the attention of different social media platforms;

It's a great way to connect with new followers;

It should be fun.

Disadvantages

Anyone can normally enter which means they might just be interested in winning something because it is free;

People might unfollow you after the giveaway, especially if they don't win;

Offering a signed copy of the book may add to the level of cost, since you'll first need to have the book sent to you (for signing) before it gets to the winner(s);

Giveaways don't necessarily lead to reviews or the winner(s) even liking your book;

Some platforms are quite strict on giveaways so clearly stating the terms and conditions is a must. Facebook's policy can be particularly stringent, especially if the giveaway involves having to like a page to enter – this may require some wording such as *'you don't have to like the page to enter, but it will help'* as opposed to *'you must like this page to enter'*.

Social Media

Most social media platforms don't usually cost anything to sign up to and post content on. They are an important consideration when it comes to book marketing in both day-to-day presence and the occasions when you are putting more effort into promoting your works.

The effectiveness of using social media to post about your work is based mostly upon following along with timing and the use of relevant hashtags. In recent times I've learned not to plug my own work that often as there are far more interesting subjects to talk about, and these will eventually attract the attention of potential readers. Remember, market yourself first, that's what you want people to invest in. There is no harm in sharing your work every now and then – though the less you do this the more social interest you'll receive in general. Nobody likes someone who just talks about themselves, and this translates to social media also. When rambling about your work, use moderation and consider promotion of your work only on occasion.

> **Top Tip:** Most social media platforms want users to stay on their site so including an external link in one of your posts may not get that much visibility. Instead put a link on your profile page and tell your following they can find it there.

Strategy

It's important to co-ordinate between the various platforms to effectively advertise your work. Combined with the Book Promotion methods covered, the modern social-media present author can rack up some good coverage and enhance that voice which craves to be heard. Although I have already mentioned it, it is worth noting that constantly sharing your own book is not really a good idea; most social media platforms will notice if you are sharing a link too often and may temporarily ban you from posting anything. I very often see authors randomly dropping their book links without any context and above all this is just bad manners. Remember social media is about being social, not sales driven.

It takes a good amount of time investment to build an engaged social media following. Like every other part of this journey the more you put in will eventually equate to what you get out. Keep going, your voice will get heard eventually.

Using your Blog

As a rule, whenever any of my titles are available for free or discount I will write a short blog post about it and publish this on the day with the relevant links. Seeing as my blog content doesn't often focus on my books, it's a potentially different way of reaching new readers, and the same should apply to you, if you have if you have a following that is constantly growing. There are also more creative ways to talk about your work through blogging and not just when the books are free. Every so often I will mention them in my regular content and I've also dedicated specific blog posts to them. Some creative ideas include:

> Creating a separate page for your books on your site with links;

Self-interviews that focus on specific works;

Five reasons to read your works;

Re-blogging reviews of your works from other bloggers;

A blurb reveal post;

A cover reveal post;

A book launch post.

The last three items are essential in my eyes because these subjects are what you should always blog about when you have a new book release coming. My best advice on blogging about your books is to start talking about them as soon as possible. Even when you are drafting, consideration should be given to sharing what you can about the project, in order to plant the seeds of promotion early to create an eventual buzz. Book releases will be covered further ahead along with a book launch timeline.

Facebook

We have covered paying for advertising and the basics of Facebook but it's important to communicate with your audience on a regular basis. Posting via your page about upcoming promotions, releases and recent reviews are good central subjects to use when talking about your own work. Never overlook your personal Facebook account when promoting work as there is always someone willing to grab a bargain book or even support you out of kindness. They are probably family or friends after all. This also extends to groups, which are a powerful tool for getting plenty of eyes on your work.

Facebook is a great vessel to harness the power that is behind word of mouth. When my first novel was released, many of my friends, even those who I hadn't seen or spoken to in some time, bought a copy. This all came about through a small group of friends who initially shared selfies of them with the paperback.

Twitter

Further ahead we will look at advanced methods of using Twitter, which is a powerful tool for book promotion even in its 'free' form, though there is an option to pay for boosting tweets – something I have never needed to do. Relevant hashtags are a must for good engagement results, that can potentially be built in a short amount of time. I tend to use Twitter as a socialising tool with fellow bloggers and authors while also sharing my blog content, but every so often I will speak about my own work. Be creative and inclusive; eventually someone will invest in you and then your work.

Instagram

Most of the content I produce on Instagram is via the Stories option, and aims to be fun while bolstering my presence. Every so often I will post a picture and some context beside a range of hashtags for maximum visibility. This can be especially useful when promoting a book at a discount as most of your followers will get a notification if you don't use Stories too often.

Where social media is concerned there are no advantages or disadvantages as it is all dependent mainly on following numbers, timing and reach. For timing it's important to research and track what time the majority of your following is online and try to aim for that moment. Hashtags and attractive visual content can greatly increase reach.

Book Marketing: Book Promotion Methods: Miscellaneous Free Advertising

THERE ARE ALSO SOME fantastic outside-the-box ways of amplifying your voice.

Book Trailers

For near enough every book I've released there has been a teaser trailer to go with it. I tend to create them as early as possible, and there are many different software programs which are easy to use, from the primitive to the more advanced.

Strategy

Using stock images, royalty free sound effects and music along with some time investment its an effective way to build some buzz around a book. In the past I have used Microsoft's basic movie maker program, but there are others that are free to download to put together a basic presentation. Trailers can look highly professional even if a complete amateur takes the time to learn a few basics in putting them together. A collection of slides and some text with a few smooth transitions can be an effective way to tease or relay what your book is about.

Trailers are also great to pin at the top of an author's social media account. Most platforms support video content for that all important first impression it could make.

There are plenty of paid services online that can also cater to your book trailer needs, although I have never paid for any and decided to take the plunge into learning myself. As long as you invest in the time to learn the basics, you can do that too.

Over the years I have developed a process to achieve this, and so here is a loose process of what a trailer should look and sound like:

A black or relevantly coloured background as the music fades in. Style dependent on genre;

Transition to textual or vocal introduction, quoting something key to the project. This should then smoothly transition to another image or can fade to black. This is the action part;

More textual/vocal description or a quote as the music builds. More action;

Dramatic sound effect or music comes to a climax as the title fades in. Cover reveal if available, or a relevant image along with text giving the release date or 'Coming Soon'. Fade image out along with music and sound.

Although this appears to be quite detailed, this process describes a teaser trailer that is less than thirty seconds long. Shorter is better, as attention spans and time is always being fought for on social media.

Book Banners

It would appear that a book cover isn't enough when displaying it on social media these days. Many authors, including myself, have put together a book banner which is basically a billboard-style display that includes a book cover and a background image that relates to the theme, along with a quote from a review or the blurb.

Strategy

My first book banners were created through Microsoft Paint, and they were an opportunity to share and quote a recent review beside the title of that book. There are many easy-to-use Photoshop-style programs online that can be used to put together an attractive, eye-catching banner. From experience, they do help sell books when done right, especially during a promo run.

As a wider strategy on social media, pictures and images normally receive better engagement than just text. Book banners work well when used as a profile picture or background and when pinned to the top of your feed much like a trailer. Including a **Call to Action** such as 'Available Now' or 'Free today only' will also aid in creating interest.

If you haven't got the patience, skills or time to learn even the basics, like anything you can pay for it online. There are even fellow authors who provide services to create banners so if you are engaging and networking you'll be able to find someone reputable to help.

Author Videos

A broad subject but certainly different to a book trailer, author videos can range in content from reciting your own work to simply talking about all things writing, or announcing a new project. There are near enough limitless subjects you can put into a simple selfie-type video that will add to your persona, and is proof you really exist and personal to the viewer, making them feel as you're speaking to them specifically. Remember this is a one-person-at-a-time deal.

Strategy

Recording yourself may seem weird, uncomfortable, or even daunting, but my advice is to just breathe and practice. Most writers are (or at least claim to be) introverts, so when it comes to the subject of talking about writing, and especially our own books, it can feel a little taboo. Ignore that feeling. It is not taboo and the world is not waiting to slap you down. Just remember to be yourself, and that any awkward pauses can be edited out. You'll be surprised how positively followers react to seeing your face so remember to keep those chin(s) up and be genuine.

Most handheld devices have built-in capabilities that can boast to be better than television studios of old, so the concept of an author video is always within reach, and the more you practice, the better – and more comfortable with it – you'll become.

Book Promotion: The Book Launch

Many of the marketing and promotion methods mentioned previously can be used for a successful book launch and that is the reason I have placed this section here, because by now you should at least be marketing yourself on social media, be actively blogging and have some knowledge of how you are going to amplify that voice of yours for people to hear.

Marketing for a book launch should begin **as soon as you start drafting the project**. At the initial stage, you should at least have a working title and concept of what the book is about. The rest can and will emerge as you work through the process, but communication with your following at the very early stages is important. Telling people that you are writing a book, or another book, is both scary and exciting because it is bound to be met with a reaction. The thing to remember is, any reaction at this stage is good. That reaction if you do get one will provide an indication to how the book might be received. If it is overall negative, then take that as a sign that perhaps some element might need rethinking.

The key to a good book launch is much like promoting a book; you need to explore as many ways as possible of telling people it exists and that begins now, so prepare well!

From the initial single mention of the project, the frequency of posts can gradually increase until, eventually, you will be using all your social media efforts to promote it. The more time you have, and the more resources you can use, the better the outcome should be.

The Book Launch Timeline

Below is a basic example of what my average book launch timeline looks like over the space of more than a year. For the sake of time reference, I have used the measure of time in months but other writers' situations may differ.

- **Month 1:** Ideas develop for a project. These ideas form into the concept that will make up a book. The title is decided and the genre is identified. Drafting begins. First mention of the project via social media – Twitter, Instagram and Facebook. A blog post is written and released relaying a basic idea of what the project is and a proposed release date is decided.

- **Month 1 to 3:** Drafting of the book continues. A teaser trailer is released through social media platforms.

- **Month 3 to 6: Drafting completed:** Celebratory mentions via social media. Editing and book cover team are organised and release date is finalised. Another blog post mentions this in some capacity. If you want to organise pre-release readers for early reviews, now would be the time to mention that.

- **Month 6 to 12:** Ramp up all levels of social media presence. Using **consistent creative content** to gradually build this, regularly blogging about several different subjects. Promote other works in series if applicable. Self-editing of the project begins.

- **Month 12 to 14:** Professional editing begins.

- **Month 15 to 16:** Book cover team begin their work. Edited manuscript is returned and agreed changes/amendments are made if you are happy. Blurb is revealed via social media via a blog post and shared across platforms.

- **Month 17:** Editing process is complete. Cover and blurb is revealed via social media including a blog post. Advanced copies given out to anyone interested in reading it and leaving a review upon launch.

  Book release organised: Arrange a Facebook event for the virtual launch and invite readers who are likely to be interested. Release a blog post announcing the date. Put together an updated teaser trailer and continue with engagement through social media. Organise some promotion with a few book promo sites who specialise in new releases. Send out a newsletter to contacts via mailing list. (If you are thinking of having the book available for pre-order this would be the time to organise, bearing in mind Amazon only allows the e-version for pre-order currently).

  Receive proof copy of the book from Amazon. Take a selfie with the book and post on various social media platforms to coincide with the publication day.

Publication day! Release a blog post. Use all social media platforms to tell followers about the release. Publish a short announcement video. Encourage pre-release readers to leave reviews and talk about it on their social media.

Of course this a brief overview and some of my books have been released in the space of a year, but in total the but the whole process is elastic; some projects might stretch a little longer while others might be shorter. This also doesn't take into account the drafting process not going so well. The point is, you should be spending some of your time reminding followers that your work is coming. There's a fine balance between talking about it too much and not talking about it enough, and that is why it's imperative to ramp up your social media presence by engaging and producing content that may not be related to the project. Stay present and explore every creative way you have of making content. Readers invest in that before they invest in your work.

Book Marketing: Book Promotion Worked Examples

"Start. And then finish."
"And that shows, like all authors I need to listen to my own advice."

– Paul Jameson,
visionary author of Nightjar and 76 and the Odd 93.

Book Promotion Worked Examples: Putting the theory into Practice

WHILE I HAVE LAID out book marketing and book promotion methods elsewhere, it's easier to visualise these through real examples. Over the years I have experienced several successful and some not-so-successful book releases and promotional runs, all of which served as learning curves and opportunities to do better next time around. This section looks to break down, analyse and share the various scenarios I have faced in the world of promoting books. These examples are in chronological order and highlight the time it takes for certain books to find success and sales. All books are a long-term investment and must be seen that way. Some are part of a wider series while others are stand-alone.

You may perceive some of these examples as repetitive and in some senses they are, because my philosophy in marketing is to stick with methods that work. You'll notice the results eventually grow and improve – time is on your side with all books. At the heart of my book promotion efforts is the free promo which serves as a great foundation for authors trying to find their audience. As someone who markets their books this way I assure you this not a one trick pony method, as should become apparent in later examples when I had more of a social media following and that all important back list.

Book Promotion Worked Examples

Book Promotion 1

Mission: To get as many downloads as possible for *Open Evening* and *Darke Blood*, both are Horror/Thriller in genre.

Date and Duration: September 2017 for 5 days, (Mon-Fri) with the final day including *Darke Blood*.

Price: Free via Amazon Kindle.

Method of Promotion:
Book Promotion websites: 4 Paid and 1 Free. 5 in total;
1 Facebook advertisement;

Mention across all social media platforms.

Books published at the time:
2

Cost:
Book Promotion sites: $60 (£43/ €50);
Facebook Advertisement: $5 (£3/ €4);
Total: $65 (£47/€54).
(Prices are in US dollars because the majority of sites I use charge in that currency. Pounds sterling and Euros included and are equivalent relative to the exchange rate at the time of writing).

Result:
701 free downloads of *Open Evening*;
12 paid downloads after the promotion ended;
144 free downloads of *Darke Blood*;
29 paid downloads after the promotion ended;
Open Evening reaches #1 in the Free Amazon UK occult charts during the promotion.

Analysis:
For a first ever book promotion run, the numbers were rather good. Downloads trickled in for the first few days of the free run and exploded to 600+ on the final day. A shorter run would have most probably generated a similar result, albeit rather more quickly due to the greater sense of urgency or need that could/would have been created. The decision to use a five-day promotion was mostly a stab in the dark, but it also gave a clear indication as to which promo sites were most effective as I used one for each of the days.

Top Tip: When it comes to book promo sites, if you want to get a clear indication as to how effective a site is, then only promote with them for that one day.

Factors for Success:
September/October is good time to promote horror and thriller books, the time of year helped massively. Two books available is better than one and this also backs up the concept of my best book promotion advice: have another available. This concept will be proven time and time again as the number of books I released increases.

Reviews in major markets before promotion:
Open Evening:
1 Amazon US review;
6 Amazon UK reviews.
Darke Blood:
3 Amazon US reviews;
3 Amazon UK reviews.

Social Media Following in September 2017:
Twitter <1k;
Facebook 250;
Blog 100;

Conclusion:
A higher social media following would have helped reach bigger numbers, but this was still an excellent promotional run with plenty of room for improvement. Book reviews increase over the lifetime of a book and the more reviews/ratings one has the more likely it will get picked up, the average star rating is mostly negligible with this

theory. Perhaps a higher quantity of reviews is something to try and improve on for the next promo.

Book Promotion 2

Mission: To promote *Open Evening* as the sequel *Cemetery House* is to be released the month after. Both are horror/thriller in genre.

Date and Duration: September 2018 for 3 days (Wed to Fri).

Price: Free via Amazon Kindle.

Method of Promotion:
Book Promotion Websites: 3 paid and 18 Free. 21 in total;
Mention across all social media platforms.

Books published at the time:
3

Cost: $38 (€31/£27).

Result:
583 Free downloads.

Analysis:
Although the quantity of promo sites used was quite high, most of them were free and this affected the overall result as their quality of reach may not have been the best. This promotion didn't quite beat the one of a year previous, though. 500+ downloads is still a great number for any book on a free run.

Factors for Success:

When advertising *Open Evening* for this run, the sequel was mentioned where possible. Many book promo sites will ask for a brief description or blurb of the book being promoted, so I took the opportunity to include that extra information.

Reviews in major markets before promotion:

1 Amazon US review;

7 Amazon UK reviews;

This is a one review improvement over a year. More reviews would have been desirable.

Social Media Following in September 2018:

Twitter <1k;

Facebook 300;

Blog 150;

Conclusion:

When this promotion took place, my following was still relatively small on all social media fronts. At the time I had three books on the market which would soon become four. This promotion was designed to build a buzz for that release. It was about this time when everything began to form into a turning point in both blogging and social media engagement. That 'wave' was coming in. The number of reviews hadn't changed apart from one more in the UK market – this is may have been a major factor that affected the number of downloads and was something that needed improvement.

BOOK PROMOTION WORKED EXAMPLES | 101

Book Promotion 3

Mission: To celebrate the first anniversary of the release of *The Teleporter*.

Date and Duration: April 2019 for 3 Weekdays (Wed to Fri).

Price: Free via Amazon Kindle.

Method of Promotion:
Book Promotion websites: 7 Free, 1 Paid. 8 in total;
1 Facebook Advertisement;
Mention across all social media platforms including a blog post.

Books published at the time:
4

Cost:
Book Promotion sites: $10 (£7/ €8);
Facebook advertisement: $10 (£7/ €8);
Total: $20 (£14/ €16).

Result:
814 Free downloads;
5 Paid ebook sales after the promotion ended;
1 paperback sale;
Reaches #1 in the Free Amazon UK Genetic Engineering chart during the promotion;
Reaches #1 in the Free Amazon Canada Humorous chart during the promotion.

Analysis:

This was an important promotion for *The Teleporter* as it led to a considerable amount of reviews, attention and general buzz. Although it had been out for a year, this promotion was the books official arrival. By this time, my social media following was bigger and there were a few authors who were looking to return the favour by leaving a review for my work. April seemed to be a good time to promote a comedy/superhero story and it sold well.

Factors for Success:

Having seen some steady and continuous social media growth during the first part of 2019 this promotion made for perfect timing. Superhero stories during this time were popular in both cinema and television which and formed part of the reason why I wrote it in the first place. It was also a departure from the last two releases, which were horror/thriller, and therefore added broader appeal through variety, opening more choice for potential readers. Being advertised as a shorter and standalone read also persuaded more readers to download it.

Reviews in major markets before promotion:

5 Amazon UK reviews.

Social Media Following in April 2019:

Twitter <2k;
Facebook 350;
Blog 250;
Instagram 200;

Conclusion:

The Teleporter had been published a year previous but officially arrived in April 2019, and thereafter came an influx of international reviews. This promotion spring-boarded my efforts and even led to high-end book promotion site BookBub accepting it for a featured deal three months later. For $20 (£14/ €16), this promotion may have been the cheapest investment considering the return that fol-lowed, by a growing social media and blogging follow-ing through **consistent creative content**. This promo also served as a learning opportunity namely that stand-alone books are great for hooking in new readers so they can test drive your writing and that the spring/summer months work well for this genre. Readers who are looking for a short, light, 'beach'-type read will generally pick up books like this one...and they did.

Book Promotion 4

Mission: To get as many discounted sales as possible for *The Teleporter* via high-end book promotion website BookBub.

Date and Duration: July 2019 for 1 weekday.

Price: $0.99

Method of Promotion: Bookbub Featured Deal – India, Australia, Canada and the UK only.

Books published at the time:
4

Cost: $86 (£62/ €71).

Result:

62 paid sales of *The Teleporter* at $0.99;

3 paid sales of *Open Evening*;

3 paid sales of *Darke Blood*, two of which were paperbacks;

1 paid sale of *Cemetery House*;

The Teleporter peaked at #2 in the Amazon Canada Humour chart.

Analysis:

Even now I'm astounded that a high-end book promo site with strict submission guidelines chose my work, but it proves that anyone with a book with the basic anatomy can do this. Selling every title I had available at the time along with the 62 sales of *The Teleporter*, made this the best day so far up to this point and yet again galvanises the concept of having a backlist. Although this promo didn't turn a profit, it did turn a huge corner in my efforts as an author and nearly saw me reach number one in Canada. Although hindsight is a wonderful thing, the results would have been a lot better if other promo sites had been used in conjunction.

Factors for Success:

Having a high-end promo site behind me was just one of the major factors that contributed to the success of this run. *The Teleporter* was already having a good year and that wave of success combined with this promo, made for a greater wave to ride. Although the US market wasn't included in the run (which was BookBub's decision), the book still made waves internationally. Not only was *The Teleporter* having a good year but the social media following on all fronts was also beginning to boom. Just mentioning that I had managed to get a BookBub featured deal began to turn heads.

Reviews in major markets before promotion:
7 Amazon UK reviews;
2 Amazon US Reviews;
1 Amazon Australia Review;
1 Amazon Canada Review;
This is a major improvement compared to the previous promo back in April of this same year.

Social Media Following in July 2019:
Twitter <2.5k;
Facebook 350;
Blog 280;
Instagram 200;

Conclusion:
What followed after this one-day promo was an increase in reviews over the next few months, and proved once again that this book is best advertised in the summer months – something I would implement again the next year. As before, authors whose works I'd reviewed were looking to return the favour along with a general buzz for the book. The only real regret from this promo is not stacking it with other sites to maximise sales – still, it stands as one of my best promotions.

Book Promotion 5a

Mission: To promote *Cemetery House* which is part of the *Order of the Following* series and get as many downloads for it as possible. The next book in that series *Darke Awakening* is due to arrive at the very end of the month.

Date and Duration: September 2020 for 2 weekdays (Thurs-Fri).

Price: Free via Amazon Kindle.

Method of Promotion:

Book Promotion Websites 2 Free, 4 Paid. 6 in total;

Utilising the *Order of the Following* book series Amazon product page;

Mention across all social media platforms including a blog post;

The use of multiple book banners displaying the free book and others in the series.

Books published at the time:

5

Cost: $125 (£90/ €104).

Result:

1,643 free downloads of *Cemetery House;*

5 paid downloads after the promo;

30 paid downloads of *Open Evening;*

20 paid downloads of *Darke Blood;*

1 paperback sale of *The Ghost Beside Me;*

Analysis:

Until this moment, *Cemetery House* had never been promoted on its own in any capacity. It proved itself well, though the revelation of this promotion was the number of sales generated by Books 1 and 2 in the series. The plan to gain a readership for the wider series by promoting the middle book seemed to work.

Top Tip: If you have written and published a series via Amazon you can set up a separate product page that lists all of those books in that series. This increases visibility while one or more of those titles are on promotion.

Factors for Success:
The main driving factor behind this promotion was the offer of a free book, but the other two books in the series were priced at 99 cents or equivalent. They sold a total of 50 copies between them which at that time was mostly an unprecedented level of paid sales for my work. Both of these books also had a quantity of reviews which boosted their chances of selling. Since the promotion was scheduled for the start of September, it tapped into the 'right time, right genre' thing and also coincided with the Labor Day weekend in the United States. This led to the majority of sales coming from US territory, which can be a very lucrative market to 'crack', and perhaps more importantly proved that investing money in producing and promoting a professional-looking book is worth the outlay.

Top Tip: When promoting a book in the series for free, pricing the others at a discount during the run will increase the chances they sell also.

Reviews in major markets before promotion:
2 Amazon UK reviews.
Social Media Following in April:

Twitter 4k;
Facebook 500;
Blog 550;
Instagram 220;

Conclusion:

This promotion was the first of two for September 2020 and led to nine Amazon US ratings for *Cemetery House* in less than a month making it a pivotal moment in gaining a readership for the *Order of the Following* series where the 4th book was now less than a month away. Considering 'CH' only had two UK reviews before this promo, the other books, both of which had way more reviews, really helped pull it along.

Book Promotion 5b

Mission: To promote *Darke Blood* which is part of the *Order of the Following* series and get as many downloads for it as possible. The next book in that series *Darke Awakening* is available for pre-order and will be published at the end of the month.

Date and Duration: Mid-September 2020 for 2 days (Fri – Sat).

Price: Free via Amazon Kindle.

Method of Promotion:
Book Promotion Websites 3 Free, 4 Paid. 7 in total;
Again, utilising the *Order of the Following* series Amazon product page;
Mention across all social media platforms including a blog post;

The use of multiple book banners displaying the free book and others in the series.

Books published at the time:
5, with number 6 (*Darke Awakening*) on pre-order.

Cost: $90 (£64/ €65).

Result:
845 free downloads of *Darke Blood;*
7 paid downloads after the promo;
12 paid downloads of *Open Evening*;
11 paid downloads of *Cemetery House*;
1 pre-order for *Darke Awakening*.

Analysis:
Yet again this promotion served to generate exposure to the wider series and picked up sales every title available within it. The biggest result was seeing a single pre-order come in for the fourth, yet-to-be-released book in the series, and that made the whole promo worthwhile. To see sales for *Cemetery House*, even though it had been available for free just a few weeks previous and seemed to show that new followers were coming in through social media.

Factors for Success:
More of the same as the previous promo, only the free book was a different title this time around. Having a range of professional-looking banners with each of the books in the series helped, along with the investment in book promo sites. Ratings had already started to come in for *Cemetery House,* which sold well along with *Open Evening*.

Reviews in major markets before promotion:
19 Amazon UK reviews;
15 Amazon US reviews;

Social Media Following in April:
Twitter 4k;
Facebook 503;
Blog 575;
Instagram 220;

Conclusion:
The second promo for September 2020 paved the way for a successful release of the fourth book in the *Order of the Following* series. Ratings for both *Open Evening* and *Darke Blood* exceeded twenty while *Cemetery House* eventually settled to nine. Eventually *Darke Awakening* released with 11 pre-orders and considering this was a new release in addition to being the fourth book in the series, I consider this to be a success.

Book Promotion 6

Mission: To promote and get as many downloads as possible for *The Teleporter* via high-end book promotion website BookBub.

Date and Duration: For 1 Saturday in early February 2021.

Price: Free via Amazon Kindle.

Method of Promotion:
BookBub Featured Deal – India, Australia, Canada the UK and this time the US;

Additional Book Promotion Websites 5 Paid and 6 Free;

Mention across all social media platforms including a blog post;

The use of multiple book banners displaying the free book and the other books which were discounted.

Books published at the time:
6

Cost: $330 (£239/ €275).

Result:
10,926 free downloads of *The Teleporter;*
37 paid downloads of *The Teleporter* the day after;
23 paid downloads of *The Teleporter* the day after that;
The Teleporter reaches Bestseller status on Amazon Canada some days later;
2 Paperback sales;
1 paid download of *Open Evening* on the day;
1 paid download of *Darke Blood* on the day;
1 paid download of *Cemetery House* on the day;
1 Paid download of *The Ghost Beside Me* on the day;
1 Paid download of *Darke Awakening* on the day.

Analysis:
A monumental success and a huge moment! After applying for a BookBub Featured Deal several times they surprisingly agreed to feature *The Teleporter* again, but this time with the US market added and the difference being it would be free. This stood as my most successful promotional run and galvanises everything that stands before this moment. On the day, and for weeks after, the number of pages read via KENP surged as a huge number of readers

discovered my books. The strength of a book promotion is what happens after and the defining moment came when *The Teleporter* reached Bestseller status over in Canada.

Factors for Success:

By the time 2021 rolled around, my social media following was engaged and the numbers were ever improving. This was especially so on Twitter. After finding out that BookBub had selected my book for a Featured Deal I took the advantage by shouting about it. A blog post explaining how I managed to get the deal while trying to help fellow authors proved successful and helped with the general buzz. Saturday proved to be a good day for promotion and social media with the numbers backing that up. Having a deal with BookBub previously kept my hopes alive and the rapport I had with them definitely helped. Recent reviews in both the US and UK helped that also.

Top Tip: For those looking to get themselves a featured deal on BookBub I would strongly suggest you submit a book that has a particular niche genre. *The Teleporter* is a comedy and there are far fewer comedy books as opposed to thrillers out there. Sometimes the applications for niche genres might be thin.

Reviews in major markets before promotion:
Amazon UK reviews: 20
Amazon US reviews: 20

Social Media Following in February 2021:
Twitter +6k;
Facebook 503;
Blog 700;

Instagram 220;

Conclusion:
Putting a book out into the world in this capacity is a rollercoaster of emotion. Soon after the promo reviews came in their droves and not all of them were praise. This is proof that the free promo is effective but not everyone is going to like it. Comedy in particular is always a little more subjective but overall, this was a highly worthy promo that helped me turn a huge corner. I can call myself a best-selling author because of it and that's marketable. A week after the promotion the ratings had exceeded fifty in both the UK and US markets with royalties flowing in from the continual KENP page reads for weeks after. This promotion stands as the best ever but every other promotion before led to this one.

Concluding Thoughts

While the free promotion is a common theme in these examples the results of a successful promo is governed mainly by time, investment of money and social media following. Effective advertising costs money and if you are serious about selling books then serious investment is needed. That doesn't always guarantee a good buy rate or even a quality readership who will go on to read your work and then then review it. Research is key and even asking fellow authors on social media will point you in the right direction.

Generally, the more reviews/ratings a book has, the better chance it has of selling and this is proven as my examples unfolded over time. Higher end book promotion sites generally lead to a better quality of readership but are sometimes harder to advertise with. Overall, I choose to promote my works on occasion as opposed to constant advertising while focusing on hooking a potential reader with one of my works and hoping they then see the others. As long as the results improve steadily over time I would say you are on the right track.

Book Reviews

"I would recommend every person who wishes to become a writer to use their free time for reading books at first. Then, such person should connect with other writers and learn from them. After that, every future writer should hire an editor."

"I would also recommend everyone to tie their ego and accept critics. I made progress in my writing because of the reviews motivated me what to fix and what to avoid."

— Kristina Gallo,
author of The Player Without Luck and The Seller of Sins.

Book Reviews: Overview

LIKE EVERYTHING ELSE IN authoring, the subject of reviews can be rather subjective. In the next few pages I am going to take a closer look into the finer details of book reviews, from dealing with negativity, through the business of them, to getting more reviews. I will also look at what goes into giving a good review, which is somewhat overlooked as a great method of promoting yourself.

When it comes to publishing a book, that work is then released into the public domain where anyone can buy it and anyone can then review it. First and foremost this is something you must be prepared to face and accept. Book reviews work a little differently to most product reviews because books are judged upon the quality of their content, whereas most other products are reviewed for their functionality and/or whether they do something effectively. Unfortunately, this does not work in favour of the author much of the time, and to be able to get something more than compliments or criticism in a review is indeed a rarity.

Most importantly when it comes to receiving book reviews one must approach them with a certain frame of mind and preparation is key.

Book Reviews: Preparing One's Mind and Dealing with Negativity

When it comes to book reviews, over the years I have come to the realisation that they have no real personal value. You cannot take them with you after leaving this existence and above all they are just a subjective opinion. Not to disparage anything that anyone has ever said in a complimentary or not so complimentary fashion towards my work, but I can only count with one hand the amount of times a review has shaped or helped my future writing. As much as I am thankful that someone liked my work, there is no actual value in being told it's good or bad.

Reviews are there to help persuade your next potential reader. They also assist in selling books because they go towards increasing the rating of a book. The more times a book has been rated – the easier it will be to sell it… but that's the only real value reviews have.

Every review, good or bad, works as proof that your book has been read. Whether or not the reader enjoyed it is irrelevant and that's the frame of mind you must take if you are to effectively deal with negativity. Even in the unlikely event that a reader states they didn't finish your book it still counts as a sale, free or fully priced. I probably don't need to focus on dealing with positivity as everyone likes being talked about in a nice fashion but eventually you will receive a review that is negative, and trust me when I say it won't be easy to deal with. The chances are if your book has a decent basic anatomy and a readable story most of the reviews will be positive and this will outweigh the negative. In every review comes opportunity to increase that book's visibility with the amount of times it has been rated at the very least. Some negative reviews can even benefit a book and stir interest.

As a rule it is considered unprofessional to respond directly to a negative review. My advice would be to not engage directly with a reviewer who has said anything negative towards your work. If it's abusive or even a direct attack to you personally there might be a case to report the review and potentially have it taken down (depending on the platform), but responding directly is not a good idea. However, there's no stopping you venting about it through blogging or even confiding in your social media following. I must stress that if you were to vent anywhere, you should take care to do so tactfully and gracefully. Social media has a potential to become toxic quickly and, as someone who has experienced this toxicity first-hand, I would advise you to sail these negative review waters with caution. On the other hand you'll be surprised how many fellow authors and followers will jump to your 'rescue' if you receive an unsavoury review. A certain one-star review of my superhero comedy novella stirred up a reaction and led to many more reviews that were positive from fellow authors. This in turn led to a high-end book promotion site BookBub accepting it for a promotion which most probably led to its overall success.

You must accept that, after publishing, the control of a book other than price or promotion is no longer in your hands. It can be a daunting and scary thought but also exciting to know anyone anywhere can take hold of your words and read them. Negative reviews will happen and any book without them either hasn't been read by many people or something suspicious is happening*. Not everyone will like what you have to say and that's okay, it will hurt less over time and the right frame of mind is ever so important in getting through negativity. Most of the time I am too busy writing something else to let reviews distract me, and above all, book reviews should not be taken personally. If you are like me then you took the plunge into writing because you enjoy the writing and storytelling part of this journey, what people think, good or bad is best described by the publishing world's favourite word; subjective.

*There is a seedy underworld of false and paid reviews online, a subject we will explore next.

Book Reviews: The Business of Reviews

LIKE MOST SALES METHODS these days, results come from creating a sense of need and convincing a potential consumer that they must have the product being advertised. The same can be said about book reviews. With the ever-growing online market for books there are millions of authors who are all seeking reviews. It is perceived that a book is only successful when it has a certain number of reviews, but no author can tell you how many reviews that is, or when they would be satisfied. That's because the chase is endless, no matter how many reviews your books get. The need for more reviews is like the dishes; they will always be there and when the urge to wash them goes away, they'll pile up. Yet again this subject needs to be approached with the right frame of mind, because reviews alone are not the measure of success for a book.

This whole section about reviews is placed much later on in the book because they simply aren't a major priority for success in authoring. For some years I felt the need to have my books reviewed on a constant basis and the sense of struggle weighed heavily on my mind. The worry about not having enough reviews will always be there if you let it. The truth is, and it has already been laid out, you don't need hundreds of reviews to sell your work. The book promo examples in the previous section prove that. Even my most successful promotion happened when the book had around 20 reviews.

Recently I put up a poll on Twitter asking fellow writers which they would prefer; 100 book sales or just a 5-star review – all of them chose the sales, which says a lot. Ask yourself the same question whenever you feel frustrated by a lack of reviews.

The perception of a constant need for reviews comes from the fact most readers don't tend to leave them, nor do they understand how much they mean to an author. This is frustrating for all authors and unfortunately something that can be turned into a business opportunity for those looking to take advantage. That frustration, in turn, leads to desperation and that is where you'll find those who will try to exploit it.

Unless it is a deemed to be reputable book reviewing platform, it's mostly perceived as unethical to pay someone to review your book. There are only a handful of paid review service providers online that are deemed as reputable, and since I don't think paying for reviews is worth exploring no providers will be named. The money you might be tempted to spend here could be better spent on promotion, which will eventually lead to reviews anyway. This is my subjective opinion, but it is one based on experience. You don't have to look far on social media to find those who are trying to make money from reviewing books, and the right entry into a search engine will reveal more. It is worth noting that there is nothing wrong with paying a reputable reviewer for their time in exchange for reading your work, as long as their opinion is their own in the review they provide.

You might eventually find yourself being approached by someone who perhaps takes an interest in you or your work and they offer a review for a fee. Ultimately it is up to you to decipher whether they are reputable or not. You should always be aware of scammers and reviewers that charge money are normally a red flag, so research is key. Amazon take fake or paid-for reviews seriously and will suspend or even ban an author if they discover you paid for a review. Over my many years of blogging I have investigated some 'reviewers' who exploit authors for extortionate amounts of money just to regurgitate the book's blurb into a review and leave a high rating. It is the responsibility of an author to tell others that there are potential scammers out there and you never know who it might help to avoid an expensive scam. Normally, if a reviewer that offers you a financial deal in exchange for a review that is too good to be true, it probably is.

Reviews are serious business mainly because authors appear to be so desperate for them, and those who are looking to exploit that financially have developed clever and covert ways to avoid detection.

A new tactic I have seen recently works by way of a third party paying a reader to leave reviews for specific books. No doubt this third party has first approached a desperate author and taken a sum of money in exchange for a review of that specific book. A percentage of that money is then passed on to the actual reviewer. This method is potentially untraceable as the third party plays no active role in leaving the review and so the author is open to punishment.

While it is sometimes wonderful to receive reviews, like I mentioned they provide no personal value and they don't always govern the sale or success of a book. Promotion of yourself and the work will do that just as effectively.

The business of reviews isn't just about those trying to take advantage of an author. There are many wonderful social network-style platforms that aim to provide readers with good books while also getting these books reviewed for authors. They know how much authors seem to need them so they take advantage of that business, albeit in a friendlier, social way that helps readers and authors alike.

Book bloggers spend hours reading just so they can leave an honest review. This is mainly because they enjoy reading and want to give something to their preferred or chosen community/communities. That struggle for reviews is universal with all authors. The best way to fight back from it is to go out into that world of books and **review fellow**

authors works yourself. Contributing to that culture of filling the gap will be rewarding, trust me.

Book Reviews: Getting More Reviews

PERSUADING SOMEONE TO READ your work is one victory but getting them to leave a review is another challenge again, though it is also one that is realistically achievable over time. Here are a range of ways you can persuade readers to leave them:

Include a Message in Your Book

Simply including a thank you to the reader for buying your book and asking them, or prompting them, to leave a review will hopefully see them do so. The request should obviously come at the beginning of a book, while the reminder or prompt will come at the end. I normally begin my author's note at the end of a book with a message about leaving a review because feedback can be difficult to find.

Ask Family and Close Friends

Family and friends are often overlooked when it comes time to 'go public' that you've written a book but, depending on your family and circle of friends, they can be hugely beneficial in spreading the word. My first reviews for *Open Evening* came mainly from close friends and family, which eventually helped it to get noticed. Don't feel guilty about approaching them; my family and friends make up some of my most loyal readers and were there for me when my social media following was non-existent.

Approaching a Book Blogger

Most book bloggers will have a website that includes a page describing what type of books they read and enjoy. Many of them are always on the lookout for new reads and book recommendations as their reviews provide consistent content.

Research is key to finding the right kind of blogger who might enjoy your work so it's always worth taking the time to check out their latest reviews and posts. If you decide they might be for you, approach them in a friendly and less of a sales approach type of way. Be personable and don't just send blanket emails to several bloggers at once. Selling books to individuals is something you need to master before selling to the masses and if you can convince book bloggers then you'll convince others too. As a rule, I would suggest offering a free e-copy of your book in exchange for a review – this is the norm when it comes to approaching book bloggers, although some insist on buying the book themselves so their review on Amazon will be verified.

Seeing as you are searching for a review it will be honest and not always positive, this must be taken into consideration when sending anyone your work. There are many different sub-strategies when trying to get a reviewer's attention; blogs with smaller followings or those just starting out will appreciate being approached, while blogs with bigger followings might also have access to a larger audience but may have stricter submission policies.

Review Swaps

There are a plethora of authors just like you, all looking to get reviewed, and plenty of them will agree to read your work and review it if you return the favour. While this sounds simple enough in theory it's not always a guarantee in practice, and some authors may also feel a need to duplicate the rating you gave for their work so what you receive may not always be a totally honest review. Some will even say Amazon frown upon this but as long as both parties are honest – which is hard to gauge – then it's okay in my eyes.

Competitive Reviewers

Believe it or not there are reviewers on Amazon who have built up quite a profile, to the point where they are quite well known. Some of these reviewers will have a rank directly next to their handle. If you can convince a reviewer like this to take on your work it's likely another one will soon appear after as they like to sometimes compete with one another. Although it can be tricky to track down high profile Amazon reviewers, it could just be a lucrative way to get more reviews.

Incentive Reviews

There are a few ways you can accumulate more reviews by offering an incentive that isn't monetary.

Many modern book covers will feature a quote from either a review of that work or an author's previous work. If you communicate with your audience that their review could potentially be quoted on the front cover of your next book that'll incite some to not only leave a review but also put considerable effort into it.

In the past I have sent a signed paperback to reviewers who have left kind words for my other works as a thank you. Sharing this on social media will generate a positive reaction that will persuade others to leave a review for your work.

Book Review Platforms/Websites

As we have previously covered, book reviews are serious business and as the sheer volume of books published is forever increasing so is the emergence of book review platforms that specialise in bringing books to readers who will review them.

After being active in the authoring and blogging arena for some time you will probably be able to name some of the more prolific platforms that are a great way of connecting your work with a potential reader. Some sites will charge a fee to showcase your work, while others will be particularly stringent with their submission policy. If your work has the basic anatomy it shouldn't have any problems being accepted, but the challenge is to then have a potential reviewer choose your work.

Just last year I was approached by popular and growing platform Reedsy Discovery to join them and review books. There are many others out there carving a new social media path in book reviewing.

Changing the long-term Culture

Putting my heavy opinion in any subject for this book may leave me open to some criticism, but I am passionate about changing the culture when it comes to book reviews – that culture being authors reading and reviewing more books by fellow authors. My reasons for this will be laid out ahead but the best way any author can get more reviews is to review other works themselves and build up a good reputation. If all of us self-published folk were to do more to support and review each other's works as a standard behaviour then the struggle would be nowhere near what it is. Reviewing books is an opportunity and one that often gets overlooked.

Book Reviews: How to Write a Great One

While I move rather close to relaying my major turning point in authoring and blogging, first we must look at giving book reviews because they are often overlooked by most authors and bloggers as a great way of promotion. How do you write a great one? We will look at that after exploring why you should write them because everything in writing revolves around motive.

Giving book reviews, in my eyes, is **just as important** as receiving book reviews, so here are the main reasons why you should consider reviewing books:

1. Book reviews make for consistent content to blog about and will get you noticed;

2. You will be reading books, that's a win on its own. But reading books goes hand-in-hand with writing them. It will help you grow as an author because you'll be conducting indirect research into how other authors tell stories;

3. Reviewing fellow authors' works is my second-best advice for promoting yourself as an author online. It's a great opportunity to connect with others who know your struggle and most of the time it will be appreciated. Over time your opinion and support for books will become respected and your profile will grow in the wider writing community. This will lead to people investing in you;

4. You should know how great it feels to receive a review for your work, go and give that feeling to others. Supporting others as you wished to be supported will go a long way.

Have I laid it on thick enough?

So many authors fail to realise the opportunity in giving book reviews. I have already mentioned that blindly sharing the link to your own work constantly will not result in sales. Be a player in the sport of writing, know what others are writing about and support it. The key to social media success is to not be an island but a continent of contribution. The best way you can give back to the literary community is to be active within it and reviewing books is the most genuine way to do so.

How to Write a Great one…

I've done my best to convince you, so let's say you've taken some of what I have said on board. Where do you start with writing a great review? Certain platforms will have different policies when it comes to writing them and this is without going into detail about star ratings.

In simple terms a great book review is an extension of the blurb while also giving just a little more away while taking care to avoid spoilers.

As a standard I tend to use the Amazon layout, that being a headline summing up the story followed by detailed text. This text consists of roughly three paragraphs and the whole review is 200 to 300 words in total. Like writing, reviews will get better the more you spend time doing them. Relaying what the book made you feel and what you enjoyed are great subjects to focus on. What was unique about it? Has the author left something out of the blurb that readers may find useful? Remember not to give away spoilers and when it comes to anything that consists of a critique it's important to do it in a way where the author can learn from it. Try to be encouraging. You are a fellow writer after all so advice coming from you has some meaning.

Top Tip: When it comes to reviews is to try and choose a book that you think you will enjoy. This can be gauged by reading the blurb and checking out the cover. Negative reviews are something you should approach with caution because writing them is not an easy task and you probably shouldn't directly share them with the author after, but my advice is the same; try to be encouraging and supportive.

When it comes to star ratings, this is something you need to decide for yourself. If I really enjoy a book it normally gets four or five stars, five being reserved for something fantastic, original or unique. Three stars is generally positive also, but with usually with something that held it back from being fantastic so the review will contain a supportive critique. I've never given a book below three stars because I've either put that book down and not finished it or because I am yet to find a book I didn't like. There is a lot of choice out there, so I am always able to choose something I know I will probably like.

Many authors receive reviews on a rare basis and it can make their day to know someone has read and reviewed their work. Most will return that gesture with social media engagement, this will contribute positively to their profile and yours. Authors reviewing fellow authors' works creates a win-win situation that will straight away become noticeable. That's exactly what happened in my case and contributed to a major turning point.

Built for Success: Turning the corner in Authoring and Blogging

"Don't give up, and never listen to anyone who tries to interfere with your dream of becoming what you want."

– Despoina Kemeridou,
author of Fated to Meet You and Mark of a Demon.

Built for Success: A Major Turning Point

I BELIEVE THAT, AS an author and blogger, if you follow the advice laid out previous to this section, one day there will be a turning point. It *will* happen, but in order to increase the chances of getting to that turning point you need to do the things that build towards it. Some day that wave of opportunity is going to come in and, if you can find a way to identify and ride it, this will carry you to success.

The feeling of things 'taking off' in one form or another differs with each individual. It might come quicker or take longer but after this section you'll know more than I did before my numbers began to increase. What's important is that you capitalise upon any turning point to increase the chances of it dictating further success. Like I said you have to ride that wave when it comes in.

It's important for me to say firstly that there are no quick fixes to getting higher blog views or a large amount of book sales. Everything I did revolves around what you should already know; persuading people to invest in you is hard work, and that hard work mostly takes the form of producing **consistent creative content**. I'm happy to admit that I fell into most of my successful moments backside first, but some happened because I worked for them and positioned myself in the right way. The wave of opportunity presented itself in my case after quite a few factors, aligned. These factors which I shall call building blocks, eventually took me to the level I am at today; a level of continued and improved growth.

So how exactly did I turn the corner in all of this? Firstly, I had to build that corner…

Building Block One

With reference to the publishing road map you'll know that somehow in 2018 I released two books in less than twelve months. The more books I released, the more my frustration grew due to lack of sales and reviews for my already published work. By the time August of that year rolled around my frustration began to boil over due to the lack of progress I've already mentioned, but also with the lacklustre number of blog views. It's worth noting that, at this time the content I blogged about was inconsistent and I roughly averaged post every ten days with just a handful of likes and views. If you blog sporadically with little consistency the views you receive will reflect that.

I decided to fight back at that frustration and, knowing how it felt to get zero book reviews, I began to offer book reviews to fellow authors. On my Hall of Information site, I created a page that advertised a review service to fellow indie authors with a few submission guidelines. I then proceeded to share that page to my Twitter following along with the various hashtags. What happened next was… a whole lot of nothing.

Most things that are worthwhile take time… New ventures especially.

It took two months for the first author to reach out and ask for a review – that being a wonderful author from South Africa who pitched her indie-published science-fiction book–and of course I took it on. Some days later I published that first review on my Hall of Information blog and immediately broke every record for views and likes I had in just hours. That was proof enough to tell me reviewing fellow authors' books was a good idea. I was fulfilling a need – remember the art of indirect selling? That wave was coming in so I had to ride it. Not only do authors need reviews but my blog followers also enjoyed reading them, and not long after that review came out more authors began to approach me. And so more reviews began to follow – I had identified and ridden that first wave towards success and, in so doing, had also put the first building block in place by beginning to produce consistent content.

The first building block had been set and I was unlocking a formula to success.

Building Block Two

Even though there was some frustration towards my own work having no reviews, those books I'd published still had some loyal supporters. These books had the basic anatomy and I'd promoted them, along with myself, on social media. Through social media my efforts as an author began to get the attention of some bloggers with a much larger followings. One particular blogger from Ireland began to support my work and efforts in 2018, which just happened to coincide with Building Block One. Her interests matched mine along with the genre in I wrote in, and so a top tip presents itself. **Find a way to connect with people who have a voice bigger than yours**. This will happen eventually if you follow what I have done.

It's quite easy to research most social media accounts to find out what someone's interests are, find your own crowd and engage. For me this just happened through engagement and being sociable, which are sometimes the same thing. Those on social media with a larger engaged following will boost your voice through word of mouth, which is still the most powerful way to advertise anything.

Soon after this awesome blogger began to support me, other bloggers with larger followings took notice of her voice and followed me also. This rolled into 2019 and while I continued with reviewing indie books, I kept producing consistent creative content that was being noticed and needed – because all authors need reviews. Remember that word, **need**. That wave was growing, and I was somehow riding it with now two blocks set.

Building Block Three

As December 2018 emerged in what was my hardest year yet I decided to take a break from social media, even though my presence back then was minimal compared to now. At this stage I had even deleted my Twitter app and Facebook followed. My social media time diminished to less than an hour every few days. My mental health improved along with my focus which was elsewhere. At this stage I had even taken time off writing just to give my mind a rest. Even though my blogging efforts branched into reviewing indie books, I still hadn't received many requests and so one evening I decided to log on to Twitter and compose a tweet, asking the wider writing community for book recommendations. I logged off and decided I would check back in a few hours.

Upon logging back in, I discovered to my alarm that I had several hundred notifications from authors sending me their book links and recommendations. By the end of that week, I had a full list of indie books that I vowed to review in 2019. That post became a key building block towards the major turning point although it is partly linked to Block One, my Twitter following instantly grew forcing me to take it a lot more seriously. I re-installed the app and began to connect with the authors who'd contacted me. I reviewed 40 indie books in 2019, something which might be the most important factor in the whole turning point. That wave of opportunity was continuing to grow, even today I still engage with authors from that popular 'comeback' tweet. Good connections can last a lifetime and this is the true beauty of social media.

Building Block Four

The first three building blocks were built and laid in quick succession, so an important foundation for the turning point was created. The next building block would take time and work to make and set into place. In the meantime, the wave of opportunity was still growing so I rode it all the way through 2019, a year which saw my blogging views explode from just under 2000 the previous year to 9000+ by the end of 2019. Led by the consistent presence of book reviews, my Hall of Information blog surpassed the 200 and then 300 follower mark in that timeframe. It was also nominated four times for blogging awards by fellow bloggers with much higher followings than me. This fourth building block was being built by the foundation of blocks one to three. Not only was I posting book reviews nearly every week but every possible idea I could fashion into material also meant that I was publishing a blog post every three days on average. This eventually resulted in a total of 162 posts for the year, which is three times as many as 2018's total of 55 posts. Building Block Four was now set in place with the other blocks.

These four main blocks not only constructed a turning point but then also pushed my following to levels far above anything I had experienced before. Everything I offered on social media was aimed at one word: need.

The Need Factor…

To sum up, much to do with this turning point revolved around offering or supplying something that others **needed**. Sales function in a similar fashion, social media presence works this way also. I'll admit some things aligned at the right time and there was even an element of luck, but when any luck came my way I still had to harness it and fashion it into something useful.

(Block One) I was consistently reviewing books via my blog – authors needed these reviews, readers who were made up of the same community enjoyed reading recommendations and some of them possibly also imagined seeing their work featured on my blog.

(Block Two) Using others' louder voices' – the mortar between Blocks One and Three was the presence of those with a higher following than me, who saw what I stood for and supported it. Through being genuine and finding my own audience, that audience – which collectively had a following far larger – then used its voice to amplify mine.

(Block Three) The tweet I put out unlocked a major insight into the way much of social media works – play to the audience and their needs. Much of my following at the time and still now was made up of writers who are looking to not only looking to connect but were also seeking reviews for an insight into writing. We will look at advanced methods of using Twitter in a few pages' time.

(Block Four) I didn't instantly get larger numbers. They happened over time. This is a major point: it takes time and a lot of consistent creative content to get noticed. Much of Block Four was dictated by blogging. Advanced methods of blogging will be covered further ahead also.

But did it work?

These building blocks only really mention my endeavours up to the end of 2019, but you can see from the graph at the start how the entirety 2020 went. Whether something is a success or not can only be seen over the long term. In this case it was, and it is the wave I have continued to ride.

Catching That Wave: Tracking Success

HALF THE REASON I was able to ride that 'wave' was because I could see it coming. All the basics of being 'successful' as a blogger and author were there; all I needed was find the audience. The same can be applied in your case; you just need to want it and do the work.

Tracking your results is imperative to catching that wave. Knowing when to strike is governed by timing and in my case, using simple terms, I put out a book review blog post that readers liked. The numbers were great so I got to work on putting another one out and repeated. Because those posts were book reviews they were an opportunity to connect with the author, which provided a good kind of engagement that kept repeating throughout 2019. This type of repetition can be adopted across all platforms, from the subjects you post about to the books you write. This of course can only be achieved after some time of trial and error, but if something gets a good reaction, do more of it.

While sales and viewing numbers don't lie there are other ways to track whether you are on the right path. Take a look at your social media feed and scroll down to the posts you put out to followers. The ones that others engage with are what you should focus more of your energy on. For beginners this will be challenging, so a good strategy early on would be to comment on others with bigger followings, explore hashtags and find your crowd. Using the basic advice from earlier does work, especially with Twitter, but don't limit yourself to one platform; variety is key to making ground on social media and remember take it slow. Don't push it or try to rush – social media takes a tactful type of psychology to get right. Enjoy the social element and take it steady.

Eventually there will come a time on your journey where those with less of a following begin to emulate you and those with a with a larger following will begin to take notice of you. This further breaks into that art of selling because you are becoming needed. That sense of need will drive engagement and eventually book sales or blog views. More importantly this will lead to the success I believe you can find.

You should know by now that success in blogging and authoring is subjective. If you celebrate it, even the little moments, it will inspire and attract others.

Those four building blocks led to me unlocking the potential of a social media presence that eventually led to book sales, book reviews and a higher number of follows across platforms. Although I'd spent more time before that turning point as an author and blogger I still managed to capitalise on that wave, which is still growing. Every day is an opportunity because not once, even now, have I ever stopped chasing better numbers. This leads us to the advanced blogging and authoring section.

Advanced Authoring and Blogging

"Be consistent. Same time, same place – writing (and blogging) is a habit, and things get better through consistent practices."

– Morgan Smith,
author of Flashbacks (An unreliable memoir of the 60s) and a Spell in the Country.

Advanced Authoring and Blogging: Dealing with Toxicity

EVEN IF YOU FOLLOW the advice before this section and do your best to conduct yourself in the finest possible way you will eventually have a bad interaction online. Unfortunately, the world of the Internet is rife with trolls and those of the unsavoury persuasion. The greater your social media presence, the higher chance you shall come across types that are best described as toxic. From those looking to get a negative reaction from you to those who are just not very nice, these types thrive off negativity and the mob culture that exists in social media.

That mob culture is most probably the ugliest part of social media. It lurks under the surface, behind a thin veil that can very easily be punctured by a bad engagement and lead to toxicity from everyone and anyone online. But even if you leave the trolls to one side, it's extremely easy to get yourself into an argument. Most of the time these can be avoided; the cause of most disagreements is either down to polarising opinions or simply being misunderstood. Sometimes it's difficult to tell what somebody really means in a tweet since tweets are limited to so many words. Miscommunication in the real world normally leads to disagreements, the same occurs online – except there is a much larger audience lurking and some are waiting to break that thin veil without thought. An online audience can become a hate mob under almost any circumstances, even if you know or believe you are right. Things can get sour even when you're only trying to defend yourself.

In some cases, the point of the argument will quickly become lost because of the comments from the crowd jumping in. This is what I call toxic undertones. The tendency of those waiting to jump in to provoke disagreement, even on subjects that you might think are none of their business. The truth is, because you are on social media – a public platform – it becomes their business simply because they are passing by. This is both unfair and fuel for the potential fire, but it is also how social media works more or less by design. While most rational types will just scroll on by, every now and then something may hit a person's nerve. Passion for a subject can often be misconstrued for aggression and conveying the right tone in so many characters can be difficult.

I have only faced the real toxicity of social media a few times and the ramifications of a bad engagement have convinced me that as an author, and blogger, I should only share and post subject matter that does not stir polarising or strong opinion or risk causing offence. While that may sound complex it's quite easy to stay out of the toxic undertones on social media, because just one bad engagement can hurt your wider following and, if you have published work, it can be targeted quite easily. In my opinion, posting about anything mentioned above is simply not worth it. You should know by now politics and the Internet have quite a terrible history; learn from the mistakes of others and try not to repeat them by staying neutral and keeping your voice reserved. Everyone is entitled to freedom of speech but that concept is heightened on the Internet which is an über-democracy that can easily get out of hand.

To deal with toxicity on social media is to totally avoid it in the first place. If you experience an unsavoury engagement, and especially if you are attacked, the best approach is to not respond, turn off notifications and if it's abuse, report it. Bad experiences on social media can not only lead to you becoming temporarily upset, but can also affect your mental health over a longer term.

Advanced Authoring and Blogging: Preserving your Mental Health

MENTAL HEALTH IS SOMETHING all we all need to talk about more. Social media has created a potentially new influence on our minds that has never really existed until now. From the struggle to achieve instant gratification and feeling like nobody is listening to your voice, all the way to the toxic undertones and outright bullying, social media is a minefield for our minds – and this is without the effect of releasing a book into the world only to have it fall on seemingly deaf ears, as well as having to contend with the possibility of someone potentially leaving a scathing review – so it is important to remember that and know when to **intervene**. While some stuff can harden our exterior, a kill or cure approach is insufficient in keeping our mental health in check.

By intervene I mean take action when the journey starts to bring you down. To many this is known as self-care. Much like how you should deal with the toxicity of social media, the wider effect of this journey can be remedied by simply stepping away and taking a break. It's okay to go dark across all social media for a while, and by that I mean not touch it for an amount of time until you feel ready. Do something else that makes you happy.

I've gone 'off the grid' numerous times during this journey and the benefits of not being in the social media rat race are huge. I even went as far as deleting all my social media apps and logged into them once a day via the browser for a month. Truthfully in that time I didn't miss a lot, so when it's getting you down ask yourself, 'Will I miss this?' If the answer is no, then step away, delete some apps temporarily and focus on something outside of the Internet and social media. During that month I even went a step further and put away my laptop to handwrite book five. Writing is the one thing I love in all of this and I found those roots without the internet or screens.

Because most of us are in the business of using our imagination to write and be creative our minds are an important tool, but that doesn't discount anyone else who is being brought down by social media – we're in this together, so we should support those who have shared that they are having a tough time and be there for them as you would hope to be able to confide in others. The best thing we can do is talk about mental health and of course the wider subject of self-care.

My advice when it comes to intervention is to take note of how long you are spending on social media as opposed to the real world. Nothing beats genuine human-to-human interaction, so turn that wi-fi off for a while and speak to someone. even an old-fashioned phone call just to talk about things will make you feel better. Social media is wonderful if used in the right way but it's only been around a few years as opposed to our evolutionary social needs.

Advanced Tweet Machine Methods

IN THEORY THE MORE followers you have on Twitter the easier it is to get even more of them. Let's say you have that larger following now. With approximate numbers aside, you've increased that following by a significant amount and along the way you've probably gained a few friends – after all that's what social media is supposed to be about. You've followed the basic tweet machine advice seen earlier in this book and now it's time to capitalise.

As your following grows larger you'll begin to attract those with less followers and even some who have a higher count than yours. That following of yours is something they perceive as useful and it is. It's been quite a while since I mentioned an important attribute outside of the trio and this is a Twitter specific one:

In order to now capitalise on that increased following you are going to have to **spend much more time** on the platform.

Perhaps you were in the habit of checking Twitter once or twice a day, or when you received notifications. Maybe you did some commenting on other peoples' posts. Now you need to take it all a lot more seriously. That time you spend on the platform needs to be utilised wisely.

To give yourself the best possible chance at advanced Twitter success you now need:

Timing – now you have a growing audience it's important to know when they will be around to engage by looking at where the majority of your following is from and which time zone, or zones, they are in. Posting something early in the morning where you are located might be the middle of the night elsewhere. A basic tip: if the majority of those you follow are currently posting and it gets engagement, then post at the same time;

To use relevant hashtags – although mentioned in the Basic section, this is just as important for constant growth and visibility. The Twitter search bar can be a powerful tool for finding relevant hashtags;

To post regular content to keep your profile relevant and engaged – in order to not get lost in the droves of literally millions of people vying for attention you're going to need to be posting regularly to stay in your follower's feed. I'm no algorithm expert, but I do know if you don't post that often your tweets will be falling on deaf ears and there is some logic to that theory. Twitter seems to push profiles that are active and engaged so regular engagement is key here;

To engage with others regularly – a way of keeping your profile visible to newcomers and established followers is to engage with tweets by commenting and being social – this is often overlooked as a way of staying 'afloat' in the rough Twitter seas.

Your content now needs to encourage engagement of the 'good' persuasion, these include:

Sharing an experience or something someone else can learn from;

A fun but inclusive tweet (this could be about near enough anything. Include your following, confide in them, be creative);

An update – share what you are doing in both authoring and blogging. Make this inclusive, add a prompt at the end asking a question;

Running a poll – asking your wider following a question and using relevant hashtags might get a good amount of engagement – I normally avoid questions that are too polarising or where the answers are opinion-based;

Sharing external content – your advanced following should coincide with everything else going on in your authoring and blogging endeavours. Some followers may even be present on other platforms too so remember to share content like blog posts, across those platforms;

Something from your day – a selfie, a picture of your pet, something visual with variety. All text all the time can be boring. Make it fun and approachable.

Above all, in order to keep your following engaged your tweets need to entertain, inspire, inform or enrich in some capacity. You also need to engage more than you have ever done. Everything you did to get that bigger following now needs to be ramped up so you also need:

To follow back, Retweet and repeat – in my view it's only good manners to return the favour in following someone back, but now you have a bigger following it's time to use it so go a step further and Retweet a new follower's pinned/recent tweet. Doing this to most new followers will in turn attract new followers and some will even return that favour;

Stay away from junk followers – most of the time you can spot these 'suspect' accounts from a mile off. Most of them will either send you an unwanted direct message upon following or tag you in something spam-like. Try to stay away from these as they have no engagement value and are mostly trying to sell something.

To tag and thank fellow followers for helping you – this is simple but mostly social way of linking your followers together in a post that lets them know you appreciate their support. I don't do this often enough, but it's important to constantly thank those who help you. Appreciate that crowd of yours;

To take part in the most recent follower/sharing fad – whether it be a follow train or an opportunity to share your links over the years these lift-type posts have taken on many forms. As a rule I don't take part in many, but I do on occasion as they are a great way to get noticed and to build up followers quickly if executed and worded in the right way;

Reply to all comments and comment on tweets more – I have mentioned this before, but probably the biggest tip I have when it comes to the tweet machine is this: When someone comments on your tweet it's time to do your best and reply with something constructive and genuine. Just liking a reply is not enough; go above and beyond to reply and be constructive/genuine when commenting on other folks' tweets. This will count as activity and push your profile to a wider audience;

Stay away from polarising or heavy opinion – my philosophy is to keep things on the lighter side mostly. Avoid heavy politics or even controversy.

Above all this, the whole tweet machine journey should be both fun and social. If either of these stops happening then something needs addressing. I don't think there is a Twitter user out there who is fully satisfied with their follower count or level of engagement and perhaps that's the key to keep going. Your following should always be on the rise, whether it's quick or gradual; you should always be trying to make it better than yesterday. Engage with others in a courteous and productive manner, be inclusive and try not to stir heavy debate and opinion, all of which is governed by the most important word in all of this: honesty.

An often-overlooked tool on Twitter is the 'Analytics' which is free and can be found in the options alongside 'Settings and Privacy' (dependent on browser or versions). This useful interface will give you a summary of your own statistics relating to engagement, profile visits, followers and much more so you can stay in tune to what's needed for growth while also figuring out the best time to post content.

Going Viral

If you spend enough time active in the Twitter arena with a larger following, eventually and just maybe you will have a post that goes viral. This has only happened once to me and it came right out of the blue. With luck out of the picture, the main reason my post went viral on Twitter was due to selecting the right trending hashtag and, of course, **timing**. With an advanced following there is a slight possibility that a post could reach thousands more than usual. In my case I unwillingly and innocently started one morning by sharing a current meme of a former US president who lost an election. It was only a few hours later that I realised this tweet had reached tens of thousands of people outside my usual demographic. This, in turn, increased views on other platforms and my Twitter profile was a lot 'hotter' during the popularity of this post, so everything I posted soon after got a higher-than-usual reception. Going viral is luck of the draw, but can be achieved through tracking trends and timing along with a more advanced following.

To conclude Advanced Tweet Machine Methods you now need to:
- Spend much more **time** on the platform.
- Post **content** regularly.
- **Engage** with others regularly.

Advanced Blogging Methods

Eventually, by way of consistent creative content your blog will experience some level of growth. It may take time, but you have to keep going. This should be pushed even further while you're riding that wave. Of course, this is all subjective, but following all the previous blogging advice and building your own turning point should eventually lead you to a bigger following. I've said this many times but **you can do it**. I know this because I did it, and the truth is, to begin with I didn't even know it was happening.

In my experience most blog followers are drawn by a particular post that spoke to them or they liked for some reason. Many of them are bloggers themselves and so in turn I followed them and began supporting their work – extending that social bridge to other bloggers is an important factor in all of blogging.

It's important to continue diversifying subject content that is both good quality and likeable in order to capture even more new followers. Keeping your existing followers is just as important and you'll know soon enough what they enjoy. Much like with the advanced tweet machine methods, you should also be able to gauge what time is best to publish your posts.

Not only do you need to practice good timing but you should also spend a lot more of it being present as a blogger by producing a lot more content. While that wave I rode was a welcome and much-loved event, it was just the beginning and over the two years that followed I kept that wave up by continually blogging to the point where my Hall of Information site became my number one platform. Today people read my blog way more than my books.

This wave started with book reviews, but they are not always going to be in large supply. It takes time to read some books. I normally post a review on average every ten days. That leaves around nine or so blog post slots to fill. This presented me with the ultimate challenge to be creative in finding things to post about, which was mainly motivated by the demand from a bigger following. Being ever-present is a huge key to success as a blogger, so here are some more advanced blogging subjects that I use quite often:

Author Interviews – a huge opportunity that is both social and promotional to both yourself and the author being interviewed. As a rule I only interview authors/bloggers whose work I have read or whose blog I follow closely, so the subject matter can be a little more researched and personable. A good interview will take time to put together, so I normally do these once or twice a month;

Book Recommendations and Monthly Review Wrap-ups – all those books I review then get mentioned further along the line in a recap post – trust me, readers like these. Some bloggers will do a monthly wrap-up post about their reviews or what is going on in their life;

Weekly Meme Share – every week I fill a post with memes and anything else fun I have found on social media.

It's a great way to stay consistent and present each week;

Book Promotion results – every time I promote one of my books I then publish the results and methods used so other authors can check which promo sites are effective to hopefully help them;

Weekly Ramble – my weekly ramble post is a diary style account of 300 to 400 words that relays what is going on in my writing world. It tends to get my best amount of views/likes and each one is standalone (this is also mentioned in the basic blogging section);

The Stories that Inspire Us – at the beginning of 2020 I was struggling to find subjects to fill my weekly quota with so every so often I would write a post about one of my favourite stories from either cinema, television, video games and of course books. We all have something that inspired us, write about it, share it passionately;

Re-blogging older posts – now your following might be larger and full of newer faces they could have missed something from the past. There are bound to be some hidden gems in your posts of years gone by. Never underestimate the power of older posts that served you well. Newer eyes will definitely appreciate them and make sure you share these re-blog's on other social media platforms;

Investigative Posts – I tend to keep any type of investigation post impartial and away from controversy but there are a range of subjects in writing that present themselves as opportunities to investigate. In the past I have covered the subject of paid book reviews, effective marketing methods and the various book platforms.

These eight subjects alone will give me nearly two weeks' worth of content, which will maintain that presence in blogging.

To conclude Advanced Blogging Methods, you need to:

- **Continue** diversifying subject content to attract new followers.
- Keep your existing followers by staying **present** – this also includes engaging with their blogs if applicable.
- Keep creating content consistently and knowing what your following likes.
- **Time** and timing – spend one and gauge the other.

Advanced Authoring: Tracking Results

It's difficult to know when an author moves from beginner to advanced in their craft, because for many this journey has no real finish line. Do you measure the advancement of an author in statistics or ability? An author might only be as good as their last release but in saying that only the individual can fully know if they have advanced in any way since they started out. A good physical measure, with ability aside, would be to track sales and reviews from one time to another.

As an example when the year 2020 started *Cemetery House* had just two reviews on Amazon UK. By the time October came it had ten ratings in the US alone and by early 2021 it had 19. That might be considered explosive growth to some, but it still took just under two years from the release date to achieve. While some might experience instant sales and reviews, the ones that take time are more meaningful.

Longevity in authoring is probably the greatest sign of success. Those who keep going, looking to improve, immersing themselves in their work and showing dedication to the craft are the ones who eventually find success.

The path to being an advanced author is based entirely on the individual. For me, you can consider yourself advanced if everything has moved forward from where you once stood. While this can be related to reviews and sales, the number of books you have brought into the world is completely and utterly more important. It justifies your growth and passion. One release is great, anything over two is fantastic!

For some years my main goal in writing was to produce more books and get better at it simply because I enjoyed it and I still do. That feeling of the wonderful unknown, just where that story will go is what I do this for. Everything after, you know by now, is subjective, but that doesn't mean we can't aim to make it the best we possibly can. Some of the advice in this book will help, but you've already built the steps that I believe you can climb otherwise you wouldn't have invested in this.

Books are a lifetime investment and will represent you long after you are gone. Remember that.

Conclusion: Everything I have learned

"The hardest thing about being an indie author is letting the world know your book exists..."
"The best thing is convincing the world one person at a time this is your dream!"

– Lee Hall,
blogger and author of Open Evening and The Teleporter.

The Conclusion: A Summary for your Reference

MY AIM ABOVE ALL is to pass on everything I've learned with hopes it gives you some success. Understandably there is a lot to absorb in this book and before I conclude everything, this is a summary in shorter form of important points we have covered for your reference.

Blogging
• Pick a brand name. Make it memorable, make it unique and make it stand out.
• Rome wasn't built in a day. Set realistic expectations and try to be social.

- Remember the anatomy of a blog post.
- Produce content regularly with subject matter that ranges.

Social Media
- Have a real profile picture. Be genuine and honest. Care about others.
- Be a person not someone who just shares links. Engage with others.
- Aim to inform, inspire, entertain or provide some level of value in your posts.
- Allow people to invest in you as a person.
- Spend more time online to get more out of it and to reach an advanced following.

Writing
- Translation of your thoughts onto the page. Dedicate time to get better and have patience in all your endeavours.
- Remember the basic anatomy of a book.
- Writing and publishing more books will sell more books.
- Carve your own roadmap. Mine was governed by the trio and time. Time is your friend.
- Do the work. Plan, but remember life and success can change those plans.

Book Promotion and Marketing
- The art of indirect selling. Promote yourself as a person first.
- Selling books isn't easy.
- Book promotion is a rabbit hole of variety. There are so many paid and free ways to inform others about your

work.
- Build a mailing list. Invest in advertising seriously to get serious results.
- Marketing for a book begins as soon as you start writing it.

Book Reviews
- Good or bad they rarely have personal value.
- Proof your work has been read which will sell it more.
- Never overlook the power of giving book reviews to fellow authors. This will build trust towards your own author and blogging brand.

Mental Health
- Try to avoid toxicity online. Practice self-care and intervene if necessary.
- Taking a break has a lot of mental health benefits.

Identify that Wave and Catch it
- Build your own blocks to success and identify when things begin to rise. Ride that rising wave by using the trio. Eventually it will happen if you just keep going.

Manage your Time
- Making time for everything ultimately governs everything. If you have that time you can do anything in authoring and blogging.

The Conclusion: Everything I have Learned

You can do this, quite simply because I did and you might even leapfrog anything I've achieved. To me that would be the dream, but in authoring and blogging the best things have come from the unexpected. Although our work might set out to create a certain emotion or feeling, that experience of how the individual interprets your work is entirely out of our hands. That is a beautiful concept. It's the 'everything else' I got from writing that gives me the most. Truthfully, it's a thrill knowing anything could come from creativity.

To be able to summarise everything I have laid out in one chapter would be quite absurd, but looking back sometimes everything about this journey has been just that. Embrace the absurdity of how far you could possibly go – dream big; it's what sets us apart from any other species. We've got this far and so here we are at the finish of a venture I hope at least one person gets something from. This is everything I have learned to be successful in both authoring and blogging on social media. After this more detailed conclusion you'll find that I have included various links to the many resources that I fashioned into blog posts over the years. Advice to refer to and draw guidance from when you've perhaps had a bad day, or even if you've had a good one. My hope is that authors and a bloggers use this book in that way and return many times for reference.

So in conclusion, what does it take to find some success in both authoring and blogging in the social media age?

The Social Factor

Outside that trio possibly the most crucial part of my success in authoring and blogging is down to the social factor of everything. That turning point and wave was governed by the presence of people approaching me in a social way. Whether it be an author looking for a review or a fellow blogger who hears my voice and sees my vision all the way to so many wonderful people who have seen something in my journey and work. All of this is based around the 'social' part of social media. I cannot stress how important and rewarding it is to review fellow authors' books which is a social activity. Every platform I am active on revolves around socialising.

Offering to Fulfil a Need

This can best be described as supporting others as you wish to be supported. In all of social media there is a common struggle to be heard and appreciated. Engaging with others in a sociable and friendly way will enrich both parties involved. Leaving a comment on someone's blog post you read might even make someone's day and possibly motivate someone to do the same for you. For authors it's quite simple, be a player in the arena. Support other authors like yourself, read their work and review it like you wish to be reviewed – this might make a fellow author's year let alone day!

You have to create a sense of need that gives people what they want, or at least allow them to feel like they are going to get what they want. Remember the art of indirect selling, which leads to…

Marketing Yourself First

Fulfilling that need by engaging or supporting others will market you as an individual, which is what you must do long before thinking about selling anything else. People will see you as genuine and if you are being honest that will lead to them investing in you. That honesty is worth more than most self-promotion methods and will lead to both book sales or blogging views/follows. Someone who invests in you will then buy your work and of course the more work you have leads into the concept of…

Consistent Creative Content

You could have guessed this was going to be included and basing everything around these three words will lead to some success eventually. The three Cs applies to both authoring and blogging. From my own experience I published six books in five years, all of which have sold regularly and have a satisfying amount of reviews. I cannot stress how important it is for an author to write more books. My Hall of Information blog regularly gets over a thousand monthly views, with nearly every post getting more likes than anything published pre-2018. All of the above has worked out because I follow the trio.

Time

This won't take off overnight, but in the unlikely chance it does I would suggest you follow suit from me and write a guidebook like this one. Everything laid out in this guide happened over years and through trial and error, all governed by the factor of time. Work now, track results later.

Lay the foundations and eventually followers/readers will help build the rest for you. That's all I did. Build that turning point through hard work – most of my building blocks are made from rolling up my sleeves and making the time to do it.

Know When That Wave is Coming

It will happen eventually so get ready to ride that incoming wave. Whether it be the right person following you with influence or an influx of new followers all the way to a growing readership, keep an ear on the ground and track those views/sales and results – then work towards them. Use them as a guide to what's next. Keep going.

Look After Your Own Mind

There is no real finish line to this journey like I have said. Maybe the trick is to constantly chase and never be satisfied, but if it starts to grind on your mental health take a step back, intervene and look after yourself. Mental health is so important for our wider health and existence, do your best to take care of it and acknowledge others who may be struggling.

Enjoy and Embrace the Journey

When I look back at those early days when I first put that the Hall of Information title on a background of dark red and along with an image of old books on a shelf, I never imagined those books by other people would eventually be swapped out for the covers of my own. Back then everything and anything could have been possible. Little did I know that unlimited possibility, and that concept is something I am just coming to terms with. Blogging and authoring presents that kind of wonder eventually.

From sharing my own feelings in that first book while fumbling around in the unknown of blogging to looking up to some truly wonderful creators and readers who inspired this journey and shaped it. Putting out that first book – a partially-biographical attempt to finally address how awful my high school days were – was fortunately well-received by friends and family. It might be the oldest ride in my book amusement park but the line is the longest still. The reason that book will always resonate with me is because it's based on something real – my own struggle. Readers can relate to real things; even in fiction they'll believe it and embrace it.

All of this was worth it for the social and creative elements. It was only after I turned around and noticed that wave coming in that I decided to be motivated. If only I knew that then what I know now, I would probably be sitting with triple the amount of success… but that doesn't matter because the journey is what I have lived for, and being needed by readers is what keeps me going, along with the freedom of creating characters, their stories and worlds.

To write is to feel and to feel is to truly be free and alive in a world that is constantly trying to confine us.

The reviews and content I put out serves a purpose and people have recently used the word 'respect' in my regard – **this is worth more than probably anything else I could ever imagine as success.**

That first blog post simply titled 'Pilot' led to where I stand today, pecking away at the keyboard, chasing the words, keeping things going, supporting others and hoping not just my work is a success but that others are too. I hope your journey is a success because there isn't a better gesture you can pay a writer than investing in their work, so from the bottom of my ink-filled heart, thank you for reading.

Writing, reading and blogging is home to me no matter where I hang my hat and you, are welcome there any time. You'll find yourself in those words if you spend long enough trying to figure it all out. When I look at a page filled with my own words it's like a mirror reflecting back at me and every essence of my feeling is in those words. It's a moment in time and for as long as that book lives so will that moment.

Not bad for a kid who found a book and got inspired. Go and find your own inspiration, reflection and feeling because all it takes is you and I might have said it too many times but **you can do this**.

Thanking Those Who Shaped This Journey

Before I share some extra resources there are a host of wonderful people who helped shape and pave the road that is my authoring and blogging journey.

None of this journey would have been possible if it wasn't for my better half, Emily. For putting up with it and of course keeping me happy – thank you.

To my brother Sean, for, those long walks and talks during those pandemic days. I needed that.

Thank you to my parents, who have always encouraged me through whatever crazy journey I've decided to embark on – this author one in particular.

To my long-term publisher and editor, Nicky who has helped shape so many of my fictional works and helped me learn ever so much about publishing.

Andrew and Rebecca from Design for Writers who have created every single cover for my works – they do some incredible work for so many authors.

To my beta-readers who were the first people to cast eyes upon this work – thank you. The work you guys put in to shape this book was above and beyond anything I'd expected. This project is that much better for your help.

Awesome blogger and friend J.C Lynch, for being one of the first people to ever believe in my work. That 2018 turning point was partly your fault – thank you.

South African Author Christina Engela, who was the first person to ever reach out to my Hall of Information blog for a review. Since then her work has featured on my blog reviews more than any other author – thank you for sending me so many of your wonderful books!

My extremely loyal Facebook following. The first folks to ever encourage me on this journey from the very early days.

To my ever growing number of fantastic, engaging and supportive followers on Twitter. I post a lot of stuff on there nearly every day and to have some wonderful folks interacting with what I say is truly special.

To those who have ever reviewed or bought one of my books. Over the years I'd like to think I've improved as a writer and storyteller which was fuelled by you.

Authors Note

Writing an authors note after a book about authoring may be a tad self-indulgent, but that's what writers are most of the time. I would like to take this opportunity to thank you for choosing to read this account and what has been a journey of learning.

As an indie creative we rely very much on every single review we can get. If you are able to make time to leave one with just a few sentences that would be massively appreciated. Thanks for reading and I hope you enjoyed the experience.

More resources can be found via my website.
leehallwriter.com

Printed in Great Britain
by Amazon